Intel Galileo Essentials

Leverage the power of Intel Galileo to construct amazingly simple, yet impressive projects

Richard Grimmett

PUBLISHING

BIRMINGHAM - MUMBAI

Intel Galileo Essentials

First published: February 2015

Production reference: 1180215

Published by Packt Publishing Ltd.
Livery Place
35 Livery Street
Birmingham B3 2PB, UK.

ISBN 978-1-78439-890-3

www.packtpub.com

Credits

Author
Richard Grimmett

Reviewers
Austin Hughes
Alan Plotko
Jason Wright

Commissioning Editor
Ashwin Nair

Acquisition Editor
Sam Wood

Content Development Editor
Mohammed Fahad

Technical Editor
Naveenkumar Jain

Copy Editors
Neha Karnani
Merilyn Pereira

Project Coordinator
Purav Motiwalla

Proofreaders
Stephen Copestake
Paul Hindle

Indexer
Rekha Nair

Production Coordinator
Shantanu N. Zagade

Cover Work
Shantanu N. Zagade

About the Author

Richard Grimmett has always been fascinated by computers and electronics from his very first programming project that used Fortran on punch cards. He has a bachelor's and master's degree in electrical engineering and a PhD in leadership studies. He also has 26 years of experience in electronics and computers. He possesses one of the original brick phones as well as a Google glass. He now teaches computer science and electrical engineering at Brigham Young University-Idaho, where his office is filled with his many robotics projects.

I would certainly like to thank my wife, Jeanne, and family for providing me with a wonderful, supportive environment that encourages me to take on projects like this. I would also like to thank my students; they show me that amazing things can be accomplished by those who are unaware of the barriers.

About the Reviewers

Austin Hughes is a software engineer with an interest in microcontrollers, embedded systems, and robotics.

Alan Plotko is a technology enthusiast with experience in developing across the full stack. He was first exposed to programming at the age of 9 when he discovered the view source code option in his browser. Coding then quickly turned into a hobby; this led to his studying computer science at the university level. Alan loves developing applications for the Web and always makes time to attend hackathons, which are typically weekend-long programming competitions where participants build projects from scratch to benefit the community. Alan's experience extends to Python development, various database technologies, including NoSQL, and frameworks for rapid application development. When he's not writing code, Alan spends his time writing stories; he is an avid writer, having previously self-published a fantasy novel.

Jason Wright is a hardware engineer in Intel's New Devices Group, where he works on projects in the area of low-power embedded and wearable computing. Previously, he worked on Galileo-based urban sensing devices within Intel Labs Europe. Jason received his BS and MEng degrees in electrical and computer engineering from Cornell University in 2012 and 2013.

Jason would like to thank his family and friends for their continued love and support.

www.PacktPub.com

Support files, eBooks, discount offers, and more

For support files and downloads related to your book, please visit www.PacktPub.com.

Did you know that Packt offers eBook versions of every book published, with PDF and ePub files available? You can upgrade to the eBook version at www.PacktPub.com and as a print book customer, you are entitled to a discount on the eBook copy. Get in touch with us at service@packtpub.com for more details.

At www.PacktPub.com, you can also read a collection of free technical articles, sign up for a range of free newsletters and receive exclusive discounts and offers on Packt books and eBooks.

https://www2.packtpub.com/books/subscription/packtlib

Do you need instant solutions to your IT questions? PacktLib is Packt's online digital book library. Here, you can search, access, and read Packt's entire library of books.

Why subscribe?

- Fully searchable across every book published by Packt
- Copy and paste, print, and bookmark content
- On demand and accessible via a web browser

Free access for Packt account holders

If you have an account with Packt at www.PacktPub.com, you can use this to access PacktLib today and view 9 entirely free books. Simply use your login credentials for immediate access.

Table of Contents

Preface

Over the last few years, a number of important technological tools have been introduced that have enabled the migration of complex electronics projects from the University or Government Lab to almost anyone's project desk. The Galileo, an inexpensive processor system by Intel, is an example of one of these toolkits. This small, inexpensive, but powerful board can be used in a wide range of projects.

But just as important as the hardware is the community of developers who not only provide help in the area of software development, but also provide hardware add-ons for the processor board itself. Still, it can be a bit intimidating to start using Galileo to build your very own projects.

This book is designed to help anyone, even those with no programming background or experience, to be successful in building both simple but also quite complex projects. It will lead you through the process step by step so that your project designs can come to life. Hopefully, this book will inspire those with the imagination and creative spirit to build those wildly inventive designs that will revolutionize the world!

What this book covers

Chapter 1, *Getting Started with the Galileo*, begins with a discussion of how to connect power and ends with a full system, configured and ready to begin connecting amazing devices and SW capabilities to fulfill almost any project.

Chapter 2, *Accessing the GPIO Pins*, shows you to how to access these pins, both input and output, so you can do all sorts of amazing things. One of the capabilities you'll need to complete your projects is a basic knowledge of how to access the GPIO pins so that you can access all sorts of additional hardware capabilities.

Chapter 3, Adding Display Functionality, shows you how the Galileo can be connected to a display so that you can both see output and also get input from a touchscreen. One of the first things you might want to do is to connect a display up to the Galileo.

Chapter 4, Controlling DC Motors, details how to control a DC motor so that the unit can drive wheels or tracks.

Chapter 5, Adding Sensors, shows you how to add IR, Sonar, and even a compass to your project.

Chapter 6, Remote Control, covers how to communicate wirelessly with your Galileo projects, as you may want to access your projects without connecting wires.

Chapter 7, Going Further with Galileo, introduces you to the Linux capabilities of the Galileo using the example of constructing a quadruped robot.

Chapter 8, Speech Output, covers how to make your project talk as an example of how to use free, open source software to add complex functionality to your projects. One of the amazing features of today's computer systems is the ability to provide output without a screen or keyboard.

What you need for this book

The most important piece of software required for the first six chapters of the book is the Galileo IDE, which is available at `https://communities.intel.com/docs/DOC-22226`. The only other software that will be required for these chapters is the software drivers associated with the hardware that you might add to your project; these will be detailed in the individual chapters themselves.

For *Chapter 7, Going Further with Galileo,* you'll need to download a version of Debian Linux available at `https://communities.intel.com/message/231688`. To burn the image to an SD card, you'll need Win32DiskImage available at `http://sourceforge.net/projects/win32diskimager/`. You'll also need a terminal emulator program; PuTTY is one such program, available at `http://www.chiark.greenend.org.uk/~sgtatham/putty/`. Finally, you'll need a control program for servos, available at `www.pololu.com/docs/0J40/3.b`.

For *Chapter 8, Speech Output,* you'll need a free, open source software package called Espeak that is available by using the command `sudo apt-get install espeak`.

Who this book is for

This book is for anyone with a little programming skill, a bit of imagination, and the desire to create their own dazzling projects. The book is designed to start by teaching beginners the basics of Galileo and how to program it. You'll tackle more and more challenging projects until you have the know-how to build your own amazing projects.

Conventions

In this book, you will find a number of styles of text that distinguish between different kinds of information. Here are some examples of these styles, and an explanation of their meaning.

Code words in text, database table names, folder names, filenames, file extensions, pathnames, dummy URLs, user input, and Twitter handles are shown as follows: "This will un-archive a set of files and directories under the `arduino-1.5.3-Intel.1.0.3` directory structure."

A block of code is set as follows:

```
qData = false; // Initialize on reset
gSerialStdPtr->begin(9600); // Receiver
gSerialTwoPtr->begin(9600); // Sender
waitForUser(5); // Give usr time to open serial terminal
gSerialStdPtr->println("XBee-Receiver-setup");
pinMode(led, OUTPUT);
```

Any command-line input or output is written as follows:

```
mv maestro-linux-100507.tar.gz\?file_id\=0J315 maestrolinux-100507.tar.gz
```

New terms and **important words** are shown in bold. Words that you see on the screen, in menus or dialog boxes for example, appear in the text like this: "Select the **Start** | **Control Panel** | **Device Manager** inside Windows."

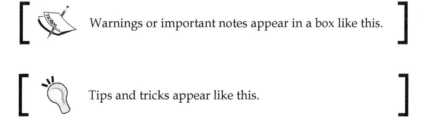

> Warnings or important notes appear in a box like this.

> Tips and tricks appear like this.

Reader feedback

Feedback from our readers is always welcome. Let us know what you think about this book—what you liked or may have disliked. Reader feedback is important for us to develop titles that you really get the most out of.

To send us general feedback, simply send an e-mail to feedback@packtpub.com, and mention the book title via the subject of your message.

If there is a topic that you have expertise in and you are interested in either writing or contributing to a book, see our author guide on www.packtpub.com/authors.

Customer support

Now that you are the proud owner of a Packt book, we have a number of things to help you to get the most from your purchase.

Downloading the color images of this book

We also provide you with a PDF file that has color images of the screenshots/diagrams used in this book. The color images will help you better understand the changes in the output. You can download this file from: https://www.packtpub.com/sites/default/files/downloads/B03435.pdf.

Errata

Although we have taken every care to ensure the accuracy of our content, mistakes do happen. If you find a mistake in one of our books—maybe a mistake in the text or the code—we would be grateful if you would report this to us. By doing so, you can save other readers from frustration and help us improve subsequent versions of this book. If you find any errata, please report them by visiting http://www.packtpub.com/submit-errata, selecting your book, clicking on the **errata submission form** link, and entering the details of your errata. Once your errata are verified, your submission will be accepted and the errata will be uploaded on our website, or added to any list of existing errata, under the Errata section of that title. Any existing errata can be viewed by selecting your title from http://www.packtpub.com/support.

Piracy

Piracy of copyright material on the Internet is an ongoing problem across all media. At Packt, we take the protection of our copyright and licenses very seriously. If you come across any illegal copies of our works, in any form, on the Internet, please provide us with the location address or website name immediately so that we can pursue a remedy.

Please contact us at copyright@packtpub.com with a link to the suspected pirated material.

We appreciate your help in protecting our authors, and our ability to bring you valuable content.

Questions

You can contact us at questions@packtpub.com if you are having a problem with any aspect of the book, and we will do our best to address it.

1
Getting Started with the Galileo

You've chosen Intel's new Galileo processor board and you are ready to start some amazing projects. However, you might be new to this kind of processor, or you might have used another similar processor but not the Galileo. This book is designed to lead you step-by-step through a number of examples that will provide you with the knowledge you need to access the power of the Galileo. You'll also learn how to add additional hardware to sense the world around you, display information, and even control motors or servos.

In this chapter, you'll start by unpacking and connecting the Galileo to your host machine, then you'll learn how to use the Galileo from your remote computer. If you know how to use Mac or Linux machines, this chapter will show you how to use them. You'll take a peek into the internals of the Galileo and learn about the Linux machine hiding behind the simple Galileo exterior.

For this chapter, the objectives are as follows:

- Unpacking and connecting the Galileo to a host computer
- Loading and configuring the Galileo IDE, based on the Arduino IDE
- Downloading and running some simple example programs
- Taking a peek at the Linux machine at the heart of the Galileo

Unpacking and connecting the Galileo

The Galileo is packaged with a power cable. Here is a picture of the board:

This is how the board will look without the adapter:

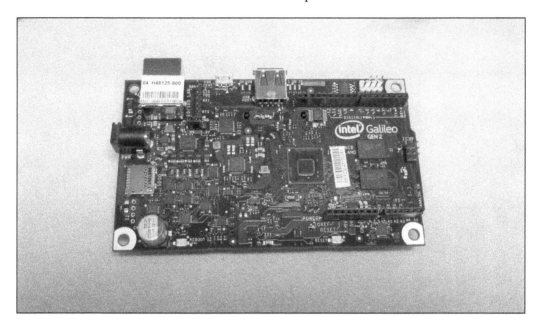

 This particular Galileo is a Gen 2 board. This version is a slightly improved version of the original Gen 1 board, and has a few connector changes. The examples in this book have been tested on both versions, and should work unless noted.

The power connection is very straightforward. However, you'll also need another cable to start working with the Galileo. This is a USB-to-micro USB cable. Here is a picture:

This cable will go between the Galileo and the host machine to develop and debug the code. Here are the specific connections:

To prepare for developing the Galileo, plug the power into an outlet and the board. A green power LED close to the USB connector should light. Now you are ready to connect your board to a remote computer to begin programming The next sections will cover how to connect your Galileo to a computer running Windows, OS X, or Linux.

Downloading the software and connecting the Galileo to a Windows machine

The first step in setting up your remote computer for development with the Galileo is to download the **Integrated Development Environment** (**IDE**) software from `https://communities.intel.com/docs/DOC-22226`. Choose the download link for Windows. This will download the IDE as well as the drivers for the Galileo. When this file is downloaded, unzip the file using an archive manager (for example 7-zip) to a location on your `C:`. This will un-archive a set of files and directories under the `arduino-1.5.3-Intel.1.0.3` directory structure.

Plug the USB from the Galileo into your computer. If you are using a newer version of Microsoft Windows, when you plug the Galileo into the system it will try to install the drivers automatically. The device will fail to install. You'll need to install the drivers manually, using the following steps:

1. Select the **Start | Control Panel | Device Manager** inside Windows. Under the **Other devices** menu, select the **Gadget Serial v2.4** device. Then select **Update Driver Software**, as shown in the following screenshot:

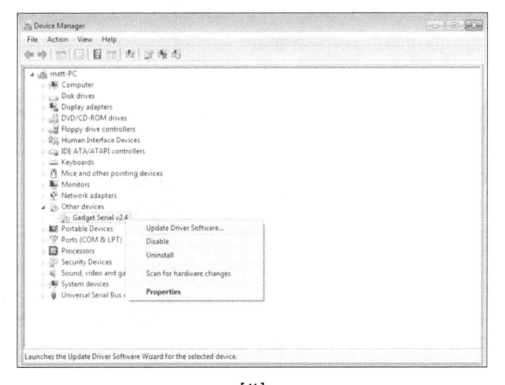

2. Next click on **Browse my computer for driver software**.

3. Click on **Browse...** next to the file path input box.

4. If you installed your Arduino IDE folder in the root of your hard drive, navigate to `C:\ardunio-1.5.3\hardware\arduino\x86\tools` and click on **OK**. If you have installed it in a different location, navigate to this directory, select it, and then click on **OK**.

You will get a security warning; click on **OK** and the drivers will install. When your drivers are installed, you should see the following device when you navigate to **Start Menu | Devices and Printers**:

In this case, the device is connected to COM port 34. Note down the COM port the Galileo is connected to as you'll need that in a minute.

Downloading the software and connecting the Galileo to a Mac

If you are using an OS X machine, download the OS X version of the IDE software at `https://communities.intel.com/docs/DOC-22226`. Unzip this file into your `Applications` folder. Then connect the 5V power to the Galileo. Connect the USB cable from the Galileo to an available USB socket on your computer. Wait for a minute while the Galileo boots up. To verify that the Galileo has loaded properly, open the **System Information** window. Then check under the **USB** tab for a **Gadget Serial v2.4** entry as demonstrated in the following screenshot:

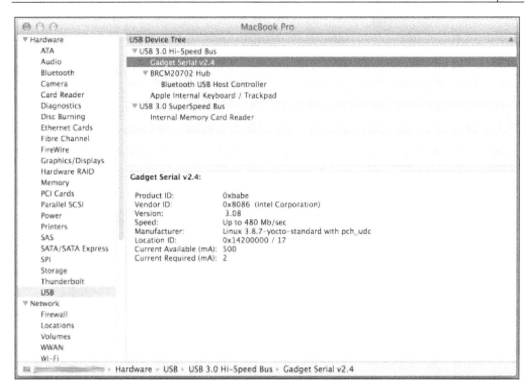

You should also check under the **Network** tab to find the device name of your Galileo. It should be something like **usbmodemXXXX**. Note down this name as you will need it to select the correct port later when you configure the connection to the Galileo. You are now ready to run the software.

Downloading the software and connecting the Galileo to a Linux machine

If you are using a Linux machine, download the Linux version of the IDE software from `https://communities.intel.com/docs/DOC-22226`. Unpack this file using `tar -zxvf arduino-1.5.3-linux32.tar.gz`. You will also need to disable the modem manager on most Linux distributions to enable uploading to the board. How you do this will vary by distribution but, if you are using the Ubuntu distribution, type `sudo apt-get remove modemmanager`.

To connect the Galileo board to the Linux machine, simply plug in the USB connector to one of the USB ports on the Linux machine. Open a terminal and `type sudo ls /dev/ttyACM*` and this will list the device connected to the machine. You should note down this value as you will later need to specify the port.

Running the IDE for the Galileo

Now that the device is installed, you can run the IDE. Select and run the program based on the type of machine you are using. The IDE should start and you should see something resembling the following screenshot:

This is the environment you will use to develop your applications. You can use this IDE to compile the code, upload it to the device, and then run it.

Setting the IDE to connect to your board

The first thing you'll need to do is set the IDE to create code for the proper Galileo board. Fortunately, the IDE lets you set that by choosing the board. To do this, navigate to **Tools | Board | Intel® Galileo Gen2**, as shown in the following screenshot:

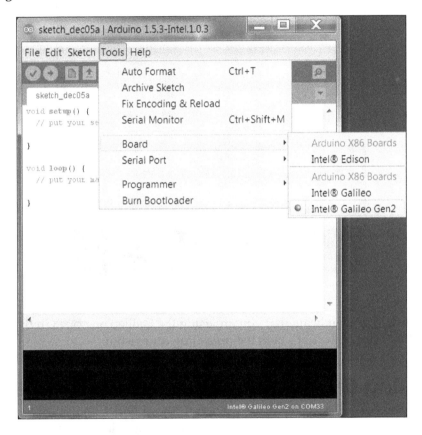

The next step, selecting a port to connect the board to the IDE, will depend on the type of operating system you are using.

Selecting the proper COM port for Windows

To specify the port for Windows, navigate to **Tools** | **Serial Port** | **COM23**, (the port you noted earlier) as shown in the following screenshot:

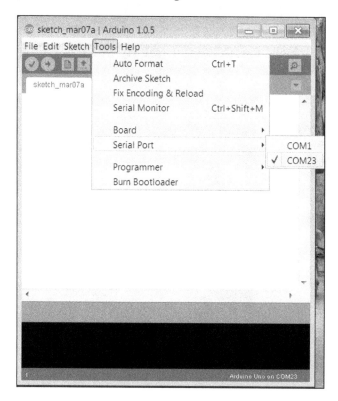

The IDE should now indicate that you are using the Galileo on COM23 in the lower-right corner of the IDE, as in the preceding screenshot.

Selecting the proper COM port for the Mac

To specify the port for Mac, navigate to **Tools** | **Serial Port** | and select the port you noted earlier when you installed the drivers. The IDE should now indicate that you are using the Galileo on the proper port in the lower-right corner of the IDE.

Selecting the proper COM port for a Linux Machine

To specify the port for a Linux machine, navigate to **Tools | Serial Port |** and select the port you noted earlier when you first connected to the board. The IDE should now indicate that you are using the Galileo on the proper port in the lower-right corner of the IDE.

Updating the firmware

The first thing you'll want to do is update the firmware on the Galileo. To do this, select **Help | Galileo Firmware Update**, as shown in the following screenshot:

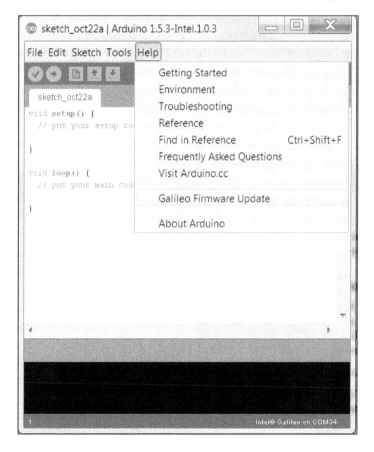

Having the latest firmware is always a good idea; you might want to repeat this step every week or so just to make sure you have the latest.

Opening and uploading a file to the Galileo

Now that your board is connected and you are running the latest firmware, you can open and upload a simple example file. It is called the blink application. It has already been written for you, so you won't need to do any coding.

To get the blink application, perform the following steps:

1. Navigate to **File | Examples | 01.Basics | Blink**, as shown in the following screenshot:

2. You should then see the Blink code in the IDE window, as in the following screenshot:

3. Select the **Upload** button, as in the following screenshot:

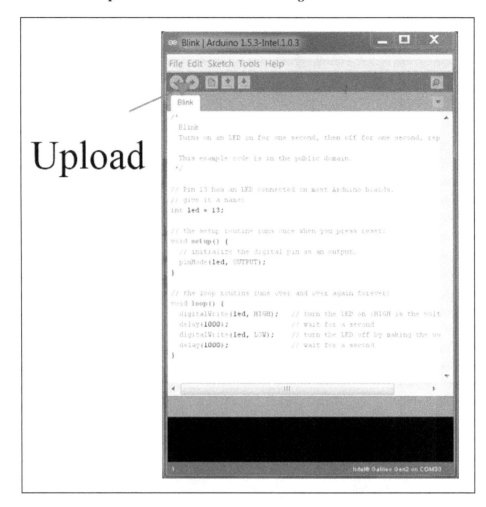

4. Once you have uploaded the file, it will tell you in the lower-left corner of the IDE display that the file is uploaded, as in the following screenshot:

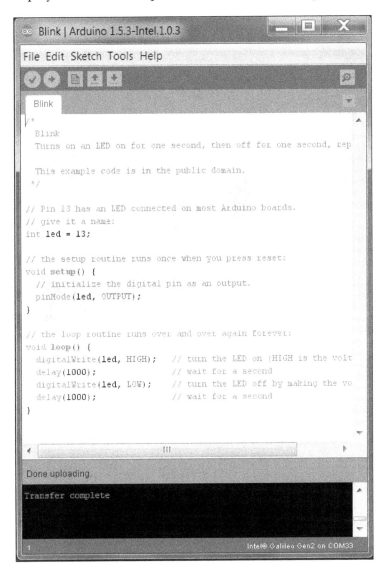

When the program is uploaded, it will automatically start running and the green LED that is positioned close to the USB connection on the Galileo will start blinking. The following images shows the LED:

You have now successfully uploaded your first program to your Galileo!

Accessing the Galileo's Linux capabilities

There are several differences between the Galileo and the more common Arduino board that many of you might be familiar with. The Galileo has significantly more processing power. However, it also starts up into a Linux operating system, and then exposes its programming environment in an Arduino-like interface. While you'll almost exclusively use the Arduino IDE interface in this book, you can also access the Linux capabilities of the Galileo. You'll learn more about this in *Chapter 7, Going Further with Galileo*.

Summary

You've completed the next stage of your journey. You have your Galileo up-and-talking with your external computer, and know how to connect to the IDE to create code. Your next step will be learning how to access the GPIO pins so that you can interact with the outside world.

2
Accessing the GPIO Pins

Now that you are familiar with the Galileo IDE and know how to create, edit, and upload a program, this chapter will now focus on hardware. You'll learn about the capabilities of the **General Purpose Input/Output** (**GPIO**) pins and how you can connect to and access them via software. Specifically, you'll learn about the following:

- The GPIO pins, what they can and can't do
- How to use and access them using some very basic circuits and very simple programming examples that demonstrate how to make the Galileo access the outside world

The GPIO capability of the Galileo

The Galileo was built to model how the Arduino accesses the outside world. Much of that access should be through the GPIO pins. The Galileo comes with a standard set of 14 digital and 6 analog IO pins, along with some additional pins to provide power and serial IO. Fortunately, the pins are actually well labeled on the board itself.

Here is a close-up:

Here is a list of pins that are available, and a brief description of what each pin can do, starting at the upper right and going clockwise. A more in-depth description of these pins will come later as you actually use them in some example projects:

Galileo Pin	Description
AREF	This pin provides a reference voltage for the analog inputs. The values on the analog pins will be reported in reference to this voltage. You'll also use this in some applications to provide a reference voltage for sensing devices. You can also provide an external reference value to this pin, which means that the numerical values of the inputs will be scaled according to the value supplied on this pin.
GND	This pin provides a ground reference for the AREF pin.
Digital (PWM~) 13/2	These 11 pins can be used to either read or write digital values. If input, the value will be read as either a 0 or 1 based on the voltage level at the input. If output, the value will be set to either a 0 or 1 based on the logic voltage level (the actual voltage will depend on the voltage logic level of your Arduino. Some are 5V logic level, others are 3.3 V logic level).

Galileo Pin	Description
Digital TX->1	This pin, and the RX pin next to it, provide a serial interface that can be used to communicate with other devices.
Digital RX->0	This pin, and the TX pin next to it, provide a serial interface that can be used to communicate with other devices.
Analog IN A5/A0	These pins do double duty. Normally, they are used as A/D inputs to the Galileo to read continuous voltage values and turn them into integer values. However, they can also be used as Digital I/O, very similar to the Digital I/O pins.
Power Vin	You can power the Galileo from this pin. This can be especially useful after you have uploaded your program. You can then disconnect the USB port and, when you apply voltage to this pin, your Galileo will boot and run the uploaded program. For the Gen1 board, this needs to be 5 volts. For the Gen2 board, you can use a voltage value from 7 to 12 Volts, so a wide variety of DC power adapter or battery configurations can be used.
Power GND	This pin would give the ground connection associated with the Power Vin connection.
Power GND	This is a ground normally associated with the Power 5V and Power 3.3V outputs.
Power 5V	This is a voltage output set to 5 Volts.
Power 3.3V	This is a voltage output set to 3.3 Volts.
RESET	This pin will reset the processor, which will cause the program to run from the beginning.
IOREF	This provides either a 3.3V, or 5 V reference, indicating the logic level of the board.

Using the GPIO pins

Now that you are aware of all the GPIO capabilities, you can start putting them to work. In order to do this, it is best to purchase a small breadboard and some jumper wires; this will make connecting to the outside world easier. Here is a picture of such a breadboard:

They are easy to find, you can purchase one at almost any electronics store, or on any electronic online sites. You'll need some jumper wires to connect from the Galileo to the breadboard. The jumper wires you want are the Male-to-Male solder-less jumper wires. Here is a picture of this sort of wire:

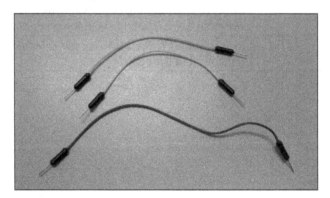

These jumper cables plug easily into the header pins on the Galileo and the breadboard. Now that you have the cables and the breadboard, you can start accessing and controlling hardware.

Connecting your first external hardware

Your first project will use the Digital IO pins to light up an LED. To do this, you'll need to gather two more hardware pieces. The first is an LED (Light Emitting Diode). This is a small part with two leads that lights up when voltage is applied. They come in a wide variety of colors. If you want to buy them online, search for a 3-mm LED. You can also get them at most electronics shops. The image shows an LED:

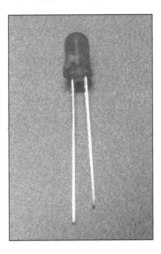

You'll also need a resistor to limit the current to the LED; a 220-ohm resister would be the right size. Again, you can get them online or at most electronics shops. The following image shows a resistor:

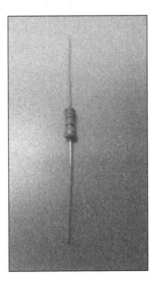

If you get three LEDs and resistors, you can exercise three of the Digital IO pins.

Plugging your wires into the breadboard

Now that you have all the bits and bobs, let's build your first hardware project. Before you plug anything in, let's look at the breadboard for a moment so that you can understand how you are going to use it to make connections. You'll be plugging your wires into the holes on the breadboard. The holes on the breadboard are connected in a unique way to make the connections you desire.

In the middle of the breadboard, the holes are connected across the board. So if you plug in a wire, and another wire in the hole right next to it, these two wires will be connected, like this:

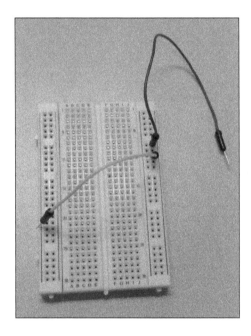

The two rows on each side of the board are generally designed to provide power, so they are connected up and down, like this:

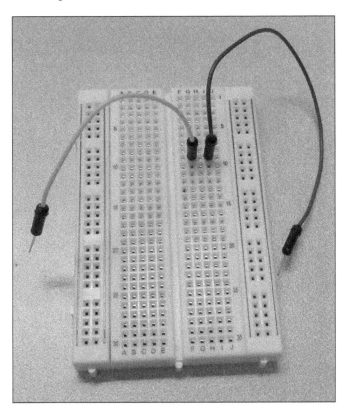

Setting up the electronics

So let's place the electronics on the breadboard. Place the LEDs in such a way that one wire is on one side of the middle split of the breadboard. The direction of the LED is important; make sure that the longer of the two wires is on the left side of the hole, like this:

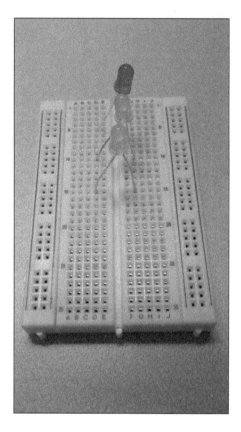

Now place the resistors on the holes on one side. The direction of the resistor does not make any difference, but make sure the second wire lead is placed in the row of holes at the end of the board, like this:

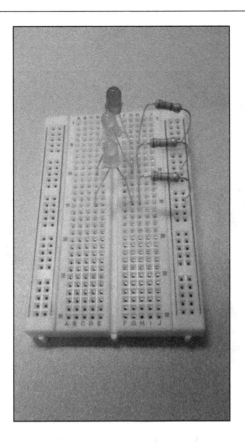

These will all be connected together, and will be connected to the GND of the Galileo using one of the jumper cables like this:

Finally, use jumper wires to connect the Digital IO pins 13, 12, and 11 to the holes on the breadboard, like this:

Now that the hardware is configured correctly, you'll need to add code to activate the LEDs.

The IDE and LED Code

To create the code for this example, start the Galileo IDE. Recall the Blink example you accessed in *Chapter 1, Getting Started with the Galileo*. The IDE should look like this:

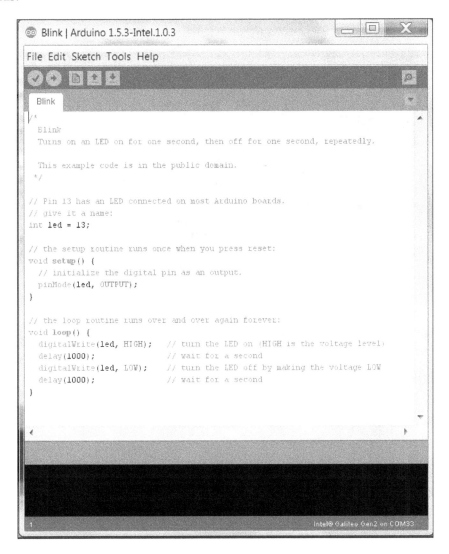

If you remember this code, `int led = 13` lit the orange LED on the board. It turns out that LED output pin 13 is also the connection to the 13 pin on the Galileo connector. If you upload and run this program, the LED connected to pin 13 should flash at the same rate as the LED on the Galileo. Here is a picture:

You'll need to add a similar bit of code to get the LEDs connected to pin 12 and 11. Add the following to the sketch on the IDE:

Here, you are replicating the code but connecting the LED connected to pin 13 to the variable led, the LED connected to pin 12 to the variable led1, and the LED connected to pin 13 to the variable led3. You then program them all to be output pins and then in the main loop toggle between high and low. Notice I have two pins toggling together (pins 13 and 11) with the other (pin 12) toggling in the exact opposite sequence. The outer two LEDs should light for one second, then the inner LED should light.

If one or more of the LEDs don't light, check to make sure they are pushed firmly down into the board. You can also change the direction of the LED; perhaps you have the leads in the wrong direction on the board.

Getting signals from the outside world

You know how to send signals to the outside world. You might also want to receive input signals from the outside world. These signals can be divided into two types: digital signals and analog signals.

Interfacing digital input signals with Galileo

There are pins on the GPIO connectors of the Galileo than can be used to sense digital input; that is, an input that will be interpreted as either a *0* or *1* by a program. These are labelled on the Galileo. An example of how to use these is a simple button press circuit. To create this circuit, you'll need one of the 220-ohm resistors you used in the LED circuit. You'll also need a simple, single-pole, single-throw switch; you can get these at most electronics stores. You'll also need some jumper wires to connect the Galileo to your circuit. Here is the circuit diagram:

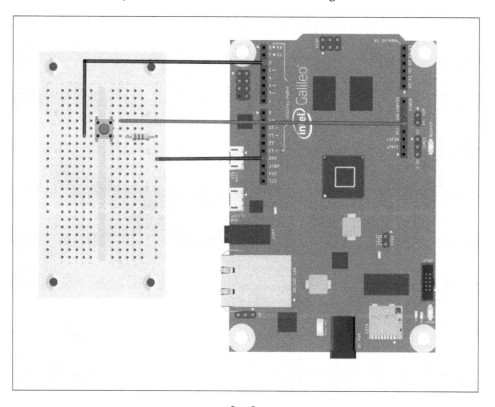

Now you'll need some code. You can use one of the example programs included with the IDE. Select the **Examples | 02.Digital | Button** code, like this:

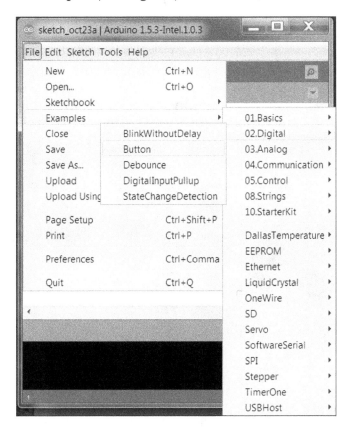

When you upload this example, you will find that pressing the button lights the LED on the Galileo board. When you release the button, the LED will not be lit. You can now get digital input into your project.

Interfacing analog input signals with Galileo

There are some signals that aren't either on, or off. You will actually want to measure the level of the signal. These are analog signals, and the Galileo can handle them as well. You'll need to use one of the analog inputs, however. These are also labelled on the board. As an example, you can build a simple electronic circuit using a potentiometer to illustrate this capability. A potentiometer is a variable resistor; you can change the resistance between two points by adjusting the potentiometer, normally by turning an adjustment either with your fingers, or a screwdriver. To create this circuit, you'll need a potentiometer, available at almost all electronics stores. Here is the circuit to build:

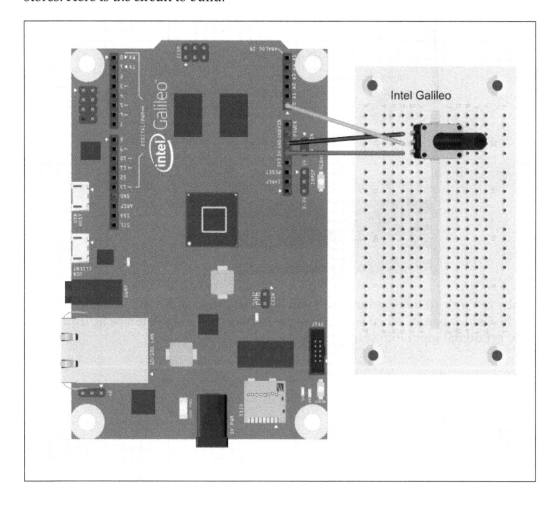

You have to connect the 5-volt connection to one side of the potentiometer, and the GND connection to the other side of the connector. The middle terminal of the potentiometer will change voltage value as you adjust the potentiometer. To measure this voltage, you'll use another example program that comes with the IDE. Select the **Examples | 03.Analog | AnalogInput**, code like this:

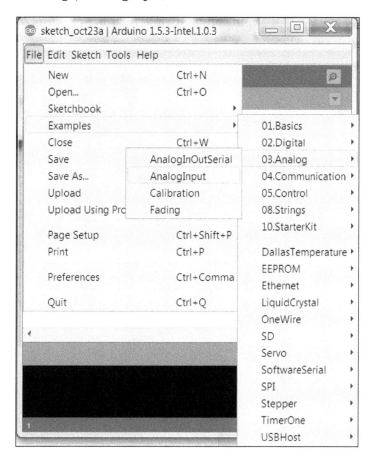

Adjusting the potentiometer will cause the LED on the Galileo to flash faster or blink more slowly. The Galileo is reading the voltage value and using that value to determine how long the LED should be on and off. You can now get analog input into your Galileo.

Summary

That's it. You've completed your very first example of interfacing with the outside world. You can play with different patterns of LED sequences by using loops and different wait states. Now that you have created your very first hardware project, in the next chapter we'll cover how to add hardware capability using a hardware shield, a piece of hardware that plugs directly into the IO connectors of the Galileo.

3
Adding Display Functionality

In *Chapter 2*, *Accessing the GPIO Pins*, you learned how to connect to the Galileo and its GPIO pins using jumper wires, breadboards, and components. In this chapter, you'll learn more about adding functionality by adding hardware designed to plug into the Galileo. In some of these examples, you'll use special hardware designed to be plugged into the Galileo's GPIO pins; these are called shields.

The simple serial display

In order to understand how to use a shield, let's start with one of the most basic display modules available for the Galileo, the serial LCD display. There are several different versions out there, but most provide a simple 2 x 16 character display that can be driven by the serial TX pin on the Arduino. They are available at most locations where the Galileo is offered. The following image shows the display:

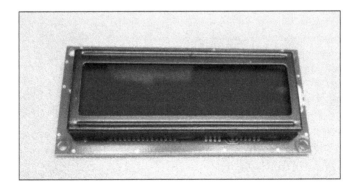

You'll need three pins to drive this display. They are a GND and VCC pin, and the TX pin. The VCC and GND will come from the 5V and GND pins on the Galileo. You'll use digital I/O pin 1 on the Galileo as a TX. To connect the Galileo to the display, connect the male to male jumpers to 5 Volts, GND, and digital input. Connect the three connectors to the proper connections on the board, like this:

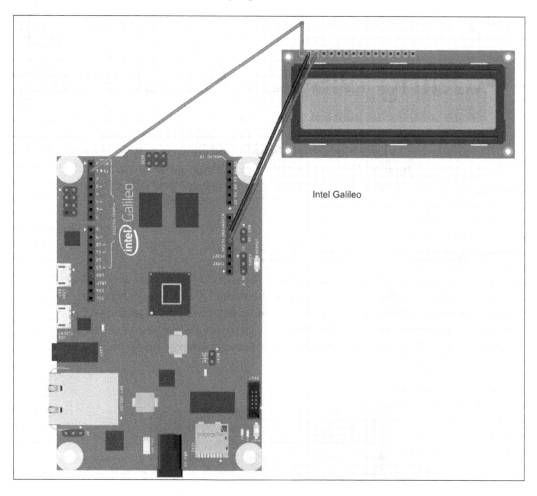

Intel Galileo

This should complete the hardware connections to the board. Now you'll need some code to write characters to the board.

Enabling the serial display in the IDE

Now bring up the IDE. Before you start coding, you'll need to get the library associated with your display and install it in the IDE. For this particular display, you'll use the serial library found at `https://github.com/downloads/nkcelectronics/SerialLCD/SerialLCD.zip`.

The `.zip` file should then exist in your **Downloads** directory. Now you'll need to place these files in the libraries directory of your DE installation. Perform the following steps:

1. To include this library in your IDE, first start your IDE and then select **Sketch | Import Library… | Add Library…**, like this:

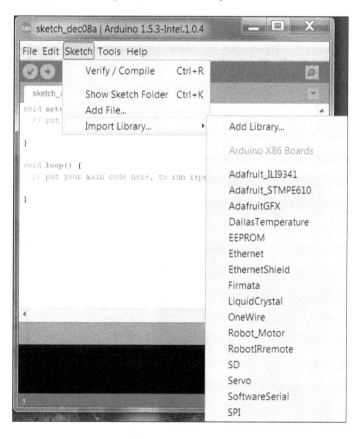

2. Now go to your **Downloads** directory and select the ZIP file that holds your library. When complete, this library should be added to your library choices. You can check this by again selecting **Sketch | Import Library… | Add Library…**like this:

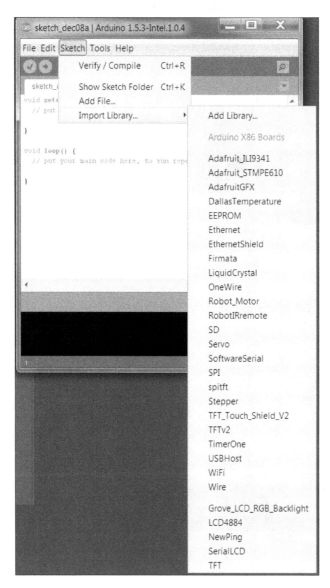

3. Once the library is installed, go back to the main IDE screen and you can write the following code:

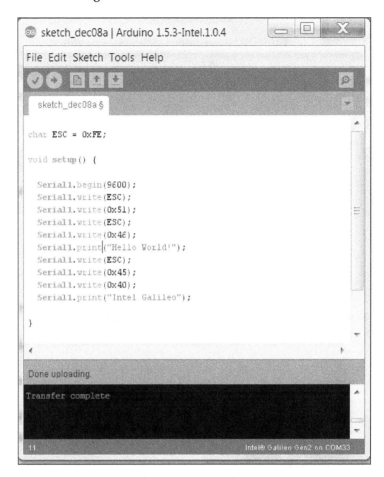

This code was written using the LCD documentation at `http://media.nkcelectronics.com/datasheet/LCM1602SK-NSW-BBW.pdf`. It is quite simple.

Lets explain the code line by line:

- `char ESC = 0xFE;` - This character needs to be sent to the display each time a command is sent

- `void setup()` - The setup function is called by the Galileo each time the program is run

- ° `Serial1.begin(9600);`:- Sets the serial port to a baud rate of 9600
- ° `Serial1.write(ESC);`:- Sends the preceding character set each time a command is sent
- ° `Serial1.write(0x51);`:- This command clears the display
- ° `Serial1.write(ESC);`:- Sends the previous character set each time a command is sent
- ° `Serial1.write(0x46);`:- Sets the cursor to the first line, the first position
- ° `Serial1.print("Hello World!");`:- Prints out Hello World!
- ° `Serial1.write(ESC);`:- Sends the preceding character set each time a command is sent
- ° `Serial1.write(0x45);`:- Sets the cursor to the second line
- ° `Serial1.write(0x40);`:- Sets the cursor to the first position
- ° `Serial1.print("Intel Galileo");`:- Prints out Intel Galileo!
- ° `void loop()`:– This loop is called over and over after the setup() function is complete

4. Now upload the sketch and you should see **Hello World! Intel Galileo** on the display, like this:

Now you can add all sorts of text. If you place a message in the loop, be sure to add in `delay(2000)`. This is a function that pauses for a number of milliseconds (in this case 2000), thus allowing the user time to read the display before it is changed.

Now you can display information from the Galileo. You might, however, want even more flexibility than this display can provide, so you'll now learn how to add a TFT display.

The TFT shield

Using a TFT display shield is another way of adding display capability to your Galileo. There is a limited set of TFT displays that will work with the Galileo and the performance isn't very fast, but it does work. First, you'll need a display, for example the Adafruit 2.8 inch TFT V2 available from `adafruit.com`. The following image shows the unit:

You'll place this shield onto the Galileo, like this:

The unit will light up and show that it is connected. Once the hardware is connected, you'll now need to access the display via the IDE.

Accessing the display with the IDE

To access the display, you'll need to follow these steps:

1. Go to the IDE libraries directory and delete the `Robot_Control` library. This has some duplicate files that will cause problems later if you don't get rid of them.

2. Download the `Adafruit_GFX` library and install it in the IDE library. You can get this library at `https://learn.adafruit.com/adafruit-gfx-graphics-library`. You'll need to unzip it, change the name from `Adafruit-GFX-Library-master` to `Adafruit_GFX` and move it into the IDE libraries directory.

3. Download a modified version of the `Adafruit_ILI9341` library from `https://github.com/wallacezq/Adafruit_ILI9341`. Unzip this library.

4. Go to the directory `Adafruit_ILI9341-master`. In that directory, you will find the `Arduino` directory and inside that directory the file `Arduino.h`. You must copy that file into the IDE at the location `\arduino-1.5.3-Intel.1.0.4\hardware\arduino\x86\cores\arduino`. Make sure you replace the existing `Arduino.h` file.

5. In the `Adafruit_ILI9341-master` directory, there is another directory named `Adafruit_ILI9341-Library`. Rename it to `Adafruit_ILI9341` and move it into the IDE libraries directory.

Now you are ready to open the IDE and an example program that will access the display. Open the **Examples | Adafruit_ILI9341 | graphicstest** example, like this:

Now upload the file using the IDE and you should see the following result:

You can now display graphics on the display! The only example from this directory that will work is the graphicstest example. The others require access to the touchscreen capability that is not yet available via the library.

Summary

That's it. You've learned how to add display capability to your Galileo projects using shields. You'll use these same concepts in later chapters to add other types of functionalities. In fact in the next chapter, you'll use the shield concept to control DC motors.

4
Controlling DC Motors

In *Chapter 3, Adding Display Functionality*, you learned how to connect to the outside world using jumper wires and specially designed hardware called shields. In this chapter, you'll learn the following:

- How to use the Galileo to control small DC motors
- How to take this to the next level, learning how to add more functionality using a shield to control the speed and direction of more powerful DC motors

DC motor basics

Before we get started with connecting everything and making it all move, let's spend some time understanding some of the basics of DC motor control. Whether you choose a two or four wheeled mobile platform, or a tracked platform, the basic movement control is the same. The unit moves by engaging the motors. If the desired direction is straight, the motors are run at the same speed. If you want to turn the unit, the motors are run at different speeds. The unit can actually turn in a circle if you run one motor forward and one backwards.

DC motors are fairly straightforward devices. The speed and direction of the motor is controlled by the magnitude and polarity of the voltage applied to its terminals. The higher the voltage, the faster the motor will turn. If you reverse the polarity of the voltage, you can reverse the direction the motor is turning in.

However, the magnitude and polarity of the voltage are not the only factor that is important when it comes to controlling your motors. The power that your motor can apply to moving your platform is also determined by the voltage and the current supplied at its terminals.

Now, there are actually GPIO pins on the Galileo that you could use to create the control voltage and drive your motors directly. The challenge with this method is that the Galileo cannot normally source enough current and voltage and thus your motors would not be able to generate enough power to move a mobile platform.

There are several solutions to this problem. The first is to use a simple transistor circuit and an external voltage source. You'll use this solution in the first example of this chapter. Another solution is to use an H-bridge, a chip that the Galileo can control but that is connected to a power source and can provide enough current. The second example in this chapter will show you how to use this sort of chip. The third solution to the problem is to use a shield that contains all the circuitry and can connect to an external power source input. Then your Galileo can provide both voltage and current so that your platform can move reliably. The last example in this chapter will use a motor controller shield designed for the Arduino to make DC motor control simple.

Connecting a DC motor directly to the Galileo

The first step in connecting a DC motor to the Galileo is to actually obtain a DC motor. The motors that you will be dealing with here are simple, small DC motors. For this example, you can use a small 6V DC motor available at most electronics or hobby stores, or online at www.amazon.com. Here is a picture of one such motor:

In order to connect this motor to your Galileo, you'll need some additional parts. You'll need two male-to-male jumper cables and two alligator clip jumper cables. You'll also need a transistor, TIP120 to be specific. You'll also need a diode, the 1N4004 diode, a 1,000-ohm resistor, and a 1 µFarad ceramic capacitor. The last four parts should be available at almost any electronics store, or online. To control this motor, you'll connect one motor connector to digital pin 11, and the other connector to GND. You could use one of the voltage sources on the Galileo, but some DC motors can draw lots of current, more than your Galileo can supply. A safer way is to connect the DC motor supply to a battery holder with 4 AA batteries.

Connect the Galileo, transistor, diode, resistor, and power supply like this:

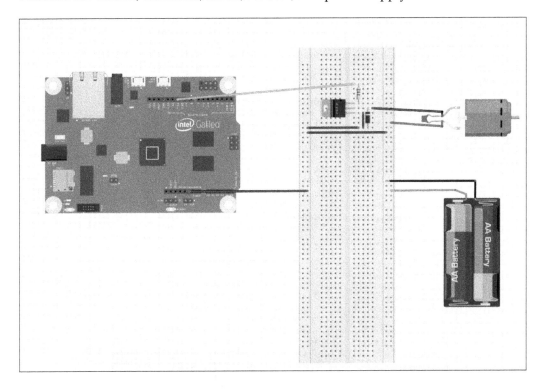

Now you can start the IDE so that you can enter a program to send a control signal to the DC motor.

Galileo code for DC motor speed control

Open the IDE and then enter the following code:

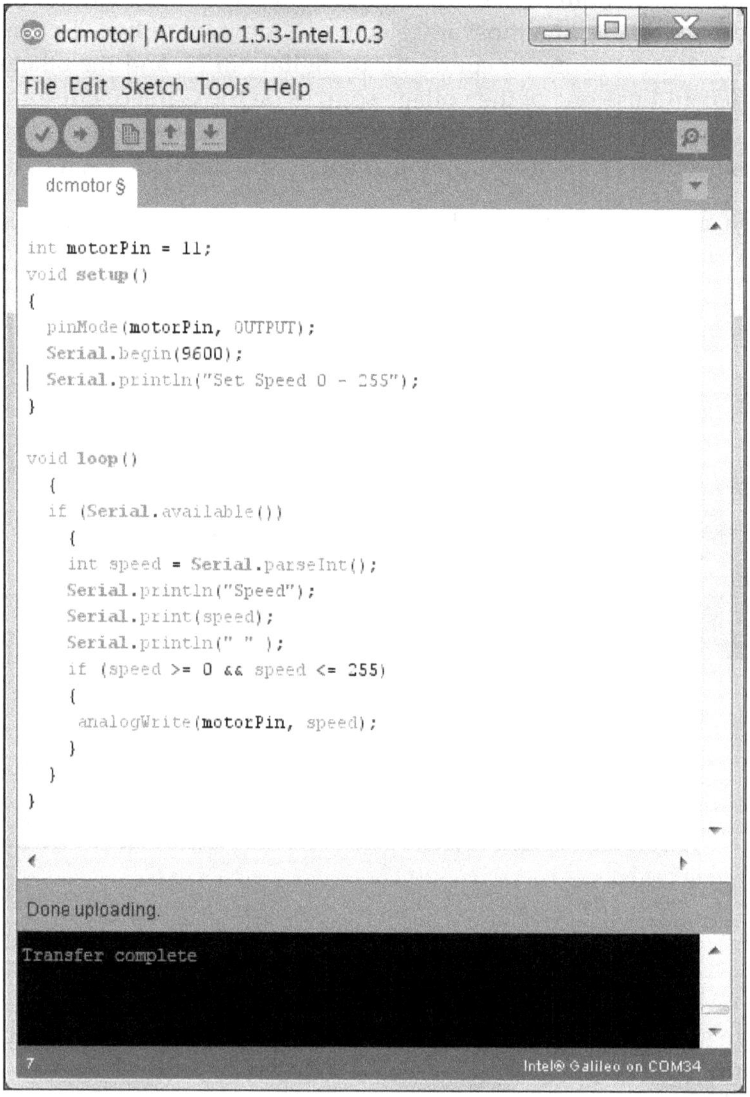

```
dcmotor | Arduino 1.5.3-Intel.1.0.3

File  Edit  Sketch  Tools  Help

dcmotor §

int motorPin = 11;
void setup()
{
  pinMode(motorPin, OUTPUT);
  Serial.begin(9600);
  Serial.println("Set Speed 0 - 255");
}

void loop()
  {
  if (Serial.available())
    {
    int speed = Serial.parseInt();
    Serial.println("Speed");
    Serial.print(speed);
    Serial.println(" ");
    if (speed >= 0 && speed <= 255)
    {
      analogWrite(motorPin, speed);
    }
  }
}

Done uploading.

Transfer complete

7                                    Intel® Galileo on COM34
```

This code sends basic commands to the Galileo to control the speed of the motor. Here are the details:

- `int motorPin = 11;` :- This sets digital I/O pin 11 to the control pin you'll be using.

- void setup():– The setup function executes once you set up your Galileo.
- pinMode(motorPin, OUTPUT);:– This sets this pin to function as an output pin.
- Serial.begin(9600);:– This starts the serial port with a baud rate of 9600.
- Serial.println("Set Speed 0 - 255");:– This prints the line "Set Speed 0 – 255".
- void loop():– This loop is performed over and over again on the Galileo.
- if (Serial.available()):– If there is a serial input date on the serial port, then do the following statements.
- int speed = Serial.parseInt();:– This brings in the data as an integer.
- Serial.println("Speed");:– This prints the line "Speed".
- Serial.print(speed);:– This prints the value input from the serial port.
- Serial.println(" ");:– This finishes the line and goes to the next line.
- if (speed >= 0 && speed <= 255):– If the speed is in the proper range, then this sends it on.
- analogWrite(motorPin, speed);:– This writes this value to the pin 11. This will set the PWM signal to the proper value to control the speed of the motor.

Now upload the code to your Galileo. Your motor should start running. Once you have uploaded the code, you'll want to open up the Serial Monitor so you can command your motor to run at different speeds. To open this, you'll select **Tools | Serial Monitor**. When you open this, you should see the following window pop up, displaying the text from your program:

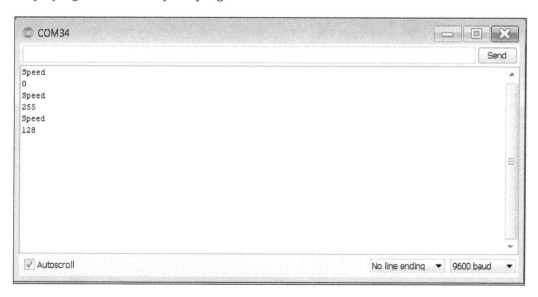

Enter a value, say 255, and then click on **Send**. Your motor should speed up. Enter another number, say 0, click on **Send**, and your motor should stop. Numbers between these two values should adjust the speed of your DC motor. Unfortunately, the motor can only go in one direction. The next example will provide a solution if you'd like bidirectional control of your DC motor.

Connecting a DC motor using an H-bridge and the Galileo

The next step is to add a bit more functionality with a new type of chip, an H-bridge. An H-bridge is a fairly simple device; it basically consists of a set of switches and functionalities to allow the direction of the current to be reversed so that the motor can either be run in the forward, or in the reverse, direction.

Let's start this example by building the H-bridge circuit and controlling just one motor. To do this, you'll need to get an H-bridge. One of the most common ones is the L293 dual H-bridge chip. This chip will allow you to control the direction of the DC motors. These chips are available at most electronics stores or online. You'll also need a capacitor; you can use the 1 µFarad from the previous example, if you like. Once you have your H-bridge, build the following circuit with the Galileo, the motor, and breadboard:

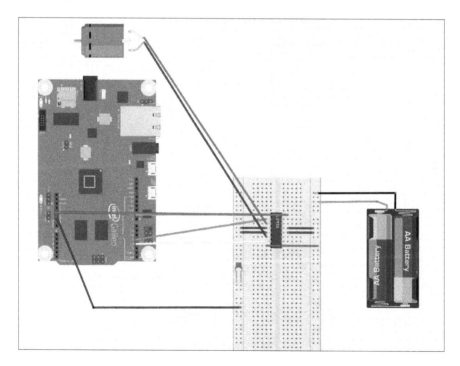

Specifically, you'll want to connect these pins on the Galileo to the pins on the H-bridge. Here is the connection list:

Galileo Pin	H-Bridge Pin
9	1
4	2
3	7

Once you have the connections, you can test the system. To do that, you'll need to add some code.

Galileo code for DC motor direction control

Open the IDE and type in the following code:

This code sets up pins 3, 4, and 9 to enable the chip and control the direction of the motor. As mentioned before, you can use the **Tools | Serial Port** to send data to the program. Sending a 0 sets pin 3 to HIGH and pin 4 to LOW, causing the motor to spin in one direction. Sending a 1 sets pin 3 to LOW and pin 4 to HIGH, causing the motor to spin in the other direction.

Now you know how to build circuits to control both the speed and the direction of DC motors. However, instead of procuring all the parts and building the circuits yourself, you can actually buy a DC motor control shield.

Controlling DC motors using a shield

For this final example, let's graduate from a simple DC motor to a wheeled platform. There are several simple, two-wheeled robotics platforms. In this example, you'll use one that is available on several online electronics stores. It is called the Magician Chassis, sourced by SparkFun. The following image shows this:

To make this wheeled robotic platform work, you're going to control the two DC motors connected directly to the two wheels. You'll want to control both the direction and the speed of the two wheels to control the direction of the robot.

You'll do this with an Arduino shield designed for this purpose. The Galileo is designed to accommodate many of these shields. The following image shows the shield:

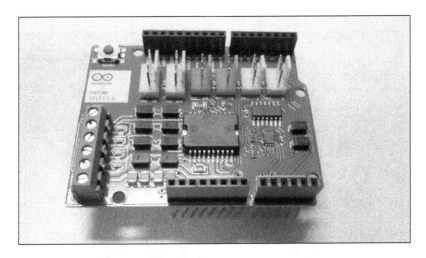

Specifically, you'll be interested in the connections on the front corner of the shield, which is where you will connect the two DC motors. Here is a close-up of that part of the board:

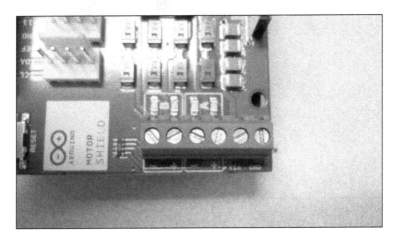

It is these three connections that you will use in this example. First, however, place the board on top of the Galileo, much as you did with the display shield from the last chapter's example. Then mount the two boards to the top of your two-wheeled robotic platform, like this:

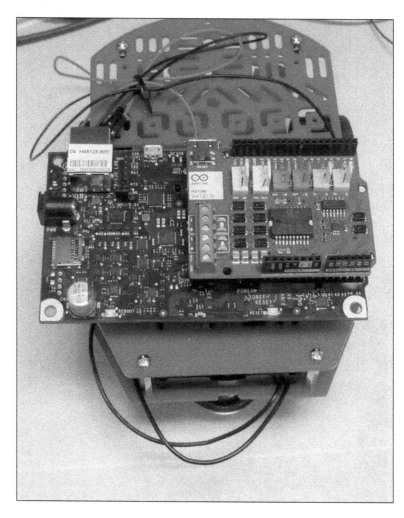

In this case, I used a large cable tie to mount the boards to the platform, using the foam that came with the motor shield between the Galileo and plastic platform. This particular platform comes with a 4 AA battery holder, so you'll need to connect this power source, or whatever power source you are going to use, to the motor shield. The positive and negative terminals are inserted into the motor shield by loosening the screws, inserting the wires, and then tightening the screws, like this:

The final step is to connect the motor wires to the motor controller shield. There are two sets of connections, one for each motor like this:

Insert some batteries, and then connect the Galileo to the computer via the USB cable, and you are now ready to start programming in order to control the motors.

Galileo code for the DC motor shield

Now that the HW is in place, bring up the IDE, make sure that the proper port and device are selected, and enter the following code:

```
int pwmA = 3;
int pwmB = 11;
int brakeA = 9;
int brakeB = 8;
int directionA = 12;
int directionB = 13;

void setup() {
  pinMode(directionA, OUTPUT);
  pinMode(brakeA, OUTPUT);
  pinMode(directionB, OUTPUT);
  pinMode(brakeB, OUTPUT);
}

void loop(){
// Move Forward
  digitalWrite(directionA, LOW);
  digitalWrite(brakeA, LOW);
  analogWrite(pwmA, 255);
  digitalWrite(directionB, LOW);
  digitalWrite(brakeB, LOW);
  analogWrite(pwmB, 255);
  delay(2000);
  digitalWrite(brakeA, HIGH);
  digitalWrite(brakeB, HIGH);
  delay(1000);
  digitalWrite(directionA, LOW);
  digitalWrite(brakeA, LOW);
  analogWrite(pwmA, 128);
  digitalWrite(directionB, HIGH);
  digitalWrite(brakeB, LOW);
  analogWrite(pwmB, 128);
  delay(2000);
  digitalWrite(brakeA, HIGH);
  digitalWrite(brakeB, HIGH);
  delay(1000);

}
```

The code is straightforward. It consists of the following three blocks:

1. The declaration of the six variables that connect to the proper Galileo pins:

```
int pwmA = 3;
int pwmB = 11;
int brakeA = 9;
int brakeB = 8;
int directionA = 12;
int directionB = 13;
```

2. The setup() function, which sets the directionA, directionB, brakeA, and brakeB digital output pins:

```
pinMode(directionA, OUTPUT);
pinMode(brakeA, OUTPUT);
pinMode(directionB, OUTPUT);
pinMode(brakeB, OUTPUT);
```

3. The loop() function. This is an example of how to make the wheeled robot go forward, then turn to the right. At each of these steps, you use the brake to stop the robot:

```
// Move Forward
digitalWrite(directionA, HIGH);
digitalWrite(brakeA, LOW);
analogWrite(pwmA, 255);
digitalWrite(directionB, HIGH);
digitalWrite(brakeB, LOW);
analogWrite(pwmB, 255);
delay(2000);
digitalWrite(brakeA, HIGH);
digitalWrite(brakeB, HIGH);
delay(1000);
//Turn Right
digitalWrite(directionA, LOW); //Establishes backward direction of
Channel A
digitalWrite(brakeA, LOW); //Disengage the Brake for Channel A
analogWrite(pwmA, 128); //Spins the motor on Channel A at half
speed
digitalWrite(directionB, HIGH); //Establishes forward direction of
Channel B
digitalWrite(brakeB, LOW); //Disengage the Brake for Channel B
analogWrite(pwmB, 128); //Spins the motor on Channel B at full
speed
```

```
delay(2000);
digitalWrite(brakeA, HIGH);
digitalWrite(brakeB, HIGH);
delay(1000);
```

Once you have uploaded the code, the program should run in a loop. If you want to run your robot without connecting to the computer, you'll need to add a battery to power the Galileo. The Galileo will need at least 2 Amps, but you might want to consider providing 3 Amps or more based on your project. To supply this from a battery, you can use one of several different choices. My personal favorite is to use an emergency cell phone charging battery, like this:

If you are going to use this, you'll need a USB-to-2.1 mm DC plug cable, available at most online stores. Once you have uploaded the code, you can disconnect the computer, then press the reset button. Your robot can move all by itself!

Summary

By now, you should be feeling a bit more comfortable with configuring HW and writing code for the Galileo. This example is fun, and provides you with a moving platform. In the next chapter, you'll change this platform from one based on DC motors to one based on servos, and you'll build a robot that can walk.

5

Adding Sensors

In *Chapter 4*, *Controlling DC Motors*, you learned how to use the Galileo to control DC motors. In this chapter, you'll learn how to add sensors to your projects. Sensors are important because you can use them to find, or avoid, objects. You can use them to sense your direction and speed, and also temperature. You can also use them to sense acoustic and electromagnetic waves, pressure, and many other physical phenomena. One of the challenges of using the Galileo is that it uses the Linux operating system at its core, so there are challenges if a sensor needs to do real— time processing of signals with tight timing. Linux is not a real-time operating system, and might be doing other things when you need to make something specific happen. This will limit some of the sensors you can use on your project. For a complete list of sensors and other hardware that are currently supported by the Galileo, see `https://communities.intel.com/docs/DOC-23423`. The goal of this chapter is to walk you through a few of the examples from this list to show you how to connect sensors to the Galileo.

Sensing distance

There are two basic sensors that will return information on the distance to an object: sonar and infrared. In the case of sonar, the sensor uses ultrasonic sound to calculate the distance to an object. The sensor consists of a transmitter and receiver, the transmitter creates a sound wave that travels out from the sensor, as illustrated here:

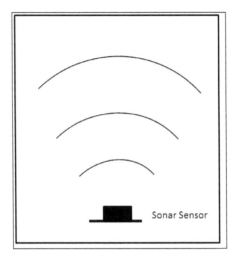

The device is triggered by an electronic signal to send out a sound wave. If an object is in the path of these waves, then the waves reflect off the object, sending waves that return to the sensor, as shown here:

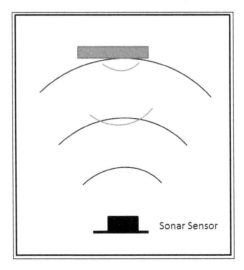

The basic sensor then measures the received sound wave and sends out an electronic signal. The user can then calculate the time difference between when the sound wave was sent out and when it returns to measure the distance to the object. Unfortunately, the return time must be measured with precision for this type of sensor to work. This is challenging for a processor such as the Galileo, that runs Linux as the base operating system. There are ways to make this work, but it is not simple. Please see the shield compatibility guide at `https://communities.intel.com/docs/DOC-23423` for details.

The Infrared sensor

Now, a little tutorial on IR sensors. The sensor you are using has both a transmitter and a sensor. The transmitter transmits a narrow beam of light, and the sensor receives this beam of light. The difference in transit ends up as an angle measurement at the sensor, as shown here:

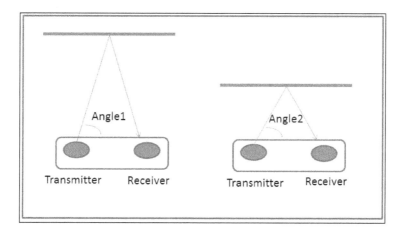

The different angles give you an indication of the distance to the object. Unfortunately, the relationship between the output of the sensor and the distance is not linear, so you'll need to do some calibration to predict the actual distance and its relationship to the output of the sensor.

The voltage to distance chart for the device looks like this:

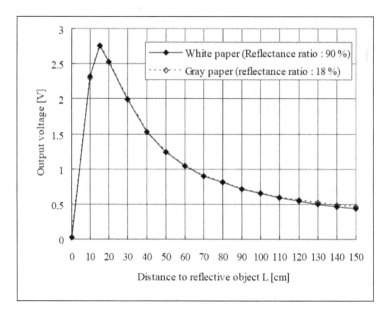

This kind of chart will come from the sensor's date sheet. There are really two parts to the curve; the first is the distance up to about 15 centimeters, then the distance from 15 centimeters out to 150 centimeters. You can simplify the code if you ignore distances closer than 15 centimeters, and model the distance from 15 centimeters and out as a decaying exponential with the form Constant * InputValue-exponential value. This will be the calculation that you will use later in the program.

Connecting an IR sensor to the Galileo

The first step in connecting an IR sensor to your Galileo is to obtain a sensor. One popular choice is the Sharp series of IR sensors. The following image shows one of the models, the Sharp 2Y0A02, a unit that provides sensing to a distance of 150 cm:

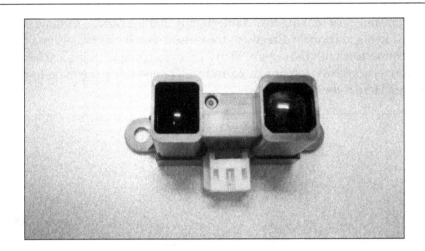

To connect this unit, you'll connect the three pins that are available on the bottom of the sensor. Here is the connection list:

Galileo Pin	Sensor Pin
5V	Vcc
GND	Gnd
A3	Vo

Unfortunately, there are no labels on the unit, but here are the pins you'll connect:

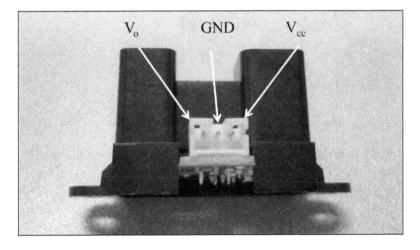

One of the challenges of making this connection is that the female-to-male connection jumpers are too big to connect directly to the sensor. You'll want to order a three-wire cable with connectors with the sensor. Many versions come with this cable. You can make the connections between this cable and the Galileo using the male-to-male jumper wires. Here is the diagram:

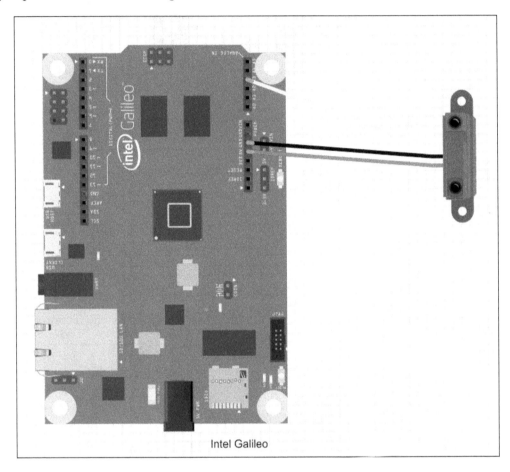

Intel Galileo

Once the pins are connected, you are ready to access the sensor via the IDE.

Accessing the IR sensor from the Galileo IDE

Now bring up the IDE. The following that provides access to the sensor and returns via the serial link the distance to the object:

This is quite simple. The three global variables at the top set the input pin to 3, and provide a storage location for the input value and distance. The `setup()` function simply sets the serial port baud rate to 9600 and prints out single line to the serial port. The Serial Monitor communicates with the Galileo via a serial port, and the baud rate specifies the communication rate between the Galileo and the host computer.

In the `loop()` function, you first get the value from the A3 input pin. The next step is to convert it to a distance based on the voltage.

If you open the Serial Monitor window and place an object in front of the sensor, you'll see the readings for the distance to the object, like this:

By the way, when you place the object closer than 15 cm, you should begin to see distances that seem much larger than indicated. This is due to the voltage-to-distance curve at these much shorter distances. If you truly need very short distances, you'll want a different sensor.

Connecting a digital compass to the Galileo

One of the important pieces of information that might be useful for your project is its direction of travel. This could be given by a GPS unit, but a GPS unit can be expensive, and it often doesn't work well inside buildings. You can also just "keep track" of the direction associated with your hardware, but you'll need to carefully update this whenever your project might move. Using a compass frees you from always having to keep track, and will also allow you to avoid inaccuracies that can accumulate from inaccuracies in your control system. So, let's learn how to hook up a digital compass to the Galileo.

There are several chips that provide digital compass capability; one of the most common is the HMC5883L 3-Axis Digital Compass chip. This chip is packaged onto a module by several companies, but almost all of them result in a similar interface. Here is an image of one by a company called SainSmart, that is available at a number of online retailers, such as www.amazon.com:

The connections to this chip are straightforward, the device communicates with the Galileo using the I2C bus, a standard serial communications bus. On the back of the module, the connections are labelled, like this:

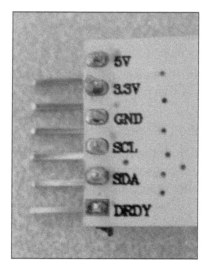

Here are the connections that you'll need to make between the Galileo and the device:

Galileo Pin	Sensor Pin
5V	5V
GND	GND
A5	SCL
A4	SDA

You won't connect to the 3.3 volt pin, as you are using the 5 volt to connect to the device. The DRDY pin is an optional connection that is used when you want to communicate at higher data rates. Now you are ready to talk with the device using the IDE.

Accessing the compass from the IDE

The first step in accessing the compass capability for the IDE is to install a library. Finding a library to support the module is a bit difficult, but the one that works well for this device is available at www.emartee.com/product/42254/HMC5883L%203%20 Axis%20Digital%20Compass%20Module.

Follow these steps to install the library and run the example:

1. Select the Arduino Library for HMC5883L link on this page and it will take you to a set of library selections.

2. You need to select the HMC5883L / HMC5883L Library for Arduino.rar link towards the bottom of this page, and this will download a .rar file that holds the library.

3. Unzip this file into the libraries directory of your Galileo IDE installation.

4. Now, bring up the IDE. If the IDE was already open, you'll want to close it and open it again so it can recognize the new library. Select **File | Examples** and you should be able to select the HMC5883L library example, like this:

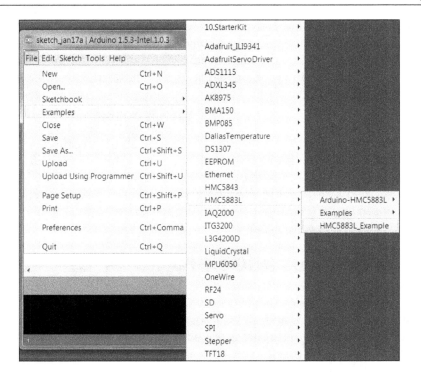

Once you have selected this example, upload it to your Galileo and open the Serial Monitor. You might have to resize the display to get a good look at the results, but you should see something like this:

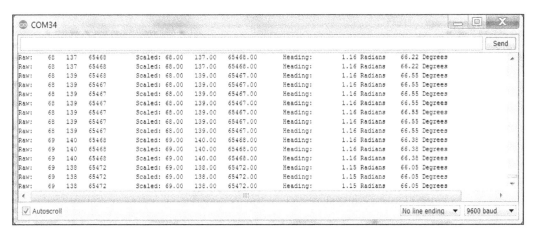

Now you can add direction to your project! As you move the device around, you should see the Heading value change. This is very useful for helping you give direction to your projects. The first three numbers are the raw magnetic sensor readings, and the middle three are angle readings from the magnet sensors. The last two are the headings in radians and degrees. The magnetic sensor is sensing the magnetic field of the earth. As you move the device around, you should see these readings change. This data can be then used to sense what direction your project is facing. The device has lots of capability, including the ability to calibrate the device so that a particular position is in the *0* position. For more information about these capabilities, feel free to look at both example programs provided by the library. However, you might want to add even more information to your project, such as the speed and tilt. Fortunately, there are sensors for this as well.

Connecting an accelerometer or gyro to the Galileo

The ability to measure speed and tilt is important in many robotics applications. This can tell you how fast your robot is traveling, and in what direction. Fortunately, there are chips that can do this for you. One of those is the **MPU-6050**, which provides a complete set of information on movement, including acceleration and tilt. For more information on this type of device, see `https://www.sparkfun.com/pages/accel_gyro_guide`. There are several different manufacturers who place this chip on a small board accessible to the Galileo. One of these is the SparkFun version, the Sparkfun SEN-11028, available at `www.sparkfun.com`. It is pictured here:

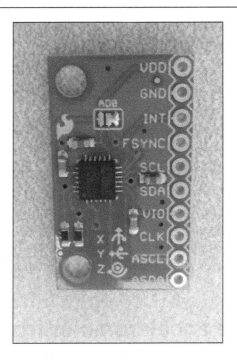

The interface to the board is quite simple, with only one issue. This particular chip will require you to solder header pins to the board to connect the jumper wires to the Galileo. You can purchase these at www.sparkfun.com as well, just search for the Arduino stackable header, the 10-pin version. Or, if you don't like to solder, you can try a solderless version, at https://www.sparkfun.com/products/10527. Once the header is connected to the board, the device will look like this:

Now you can use male-to-male jumper cable to connect the Galileo and the board. Here is the table for the connections:

Galileo Pin	Sensor Pin
3.3V	VDD
GND	GND
A5	SCL
A4	SDA
3.3V	VIO

You'll notice that you need to make two connections to the 3.3V supply, so you might want to create a male-to-male jumper cable with two connections on one end. This can be done by using two male-to-male cables, by cutting off one end and stripping back the insulation, soldering the three cables together, and then wrapping the solder connection in electrical tape.

Accessing the accelerometer from the IDE

Now that the two devices are connected, you'll need to bring up the IDE and add a library so that you can access the functionality from the SW. To get the libraries, do the following steps:

 From the Sparkfun page on the device at www.sparkfun.com/products/11028 you'll find a github repository that supports not only this device, but a number of devices that use the I2C interface.

1. Go to https://github.com/jrowberg/i2cdevlib and look on the right side of the page for the download link. This will download the entire library.

2. Now you should unzip the file to a handy location, I unzipped mine in the download directory. What you want is just the files associated with the Arduino, so go to the directory that supports those files, like this:

Downloads ▸ i2cdevlib-master ▸ i2cdevlib-master ▸ Arduino ▸		
Share with ▾ Burn New folder		
Name	Date modified	Type
_Stub	4/23/2014 4:56 PM	File folder
AD7746	4/23/2014 4:56 PM	File folder
ADS1115	4/23/2014 4:56 PM	File folder
ADXL345	4/23/2014 4:56 PM	File folder
AK8975	4/23/2014 4:56 PM	File folder
BMA150	4/23/2014 4:56 PM	File folder
BMP085	4/23/2014 4:56 PM	File folder
DS1307	4/23/2014 4:56 PM	File folder
HMC5843	4/23/2014 4:56 PM	File folder
HMC5883L	4/23/2014 4:56 PM	File folder
I2Cdev	4/23/2014 4:56 PM	File folder
IAQ2000	4/23/2014 4:56 PM	File folder
ITG3200	4/23/2014 4:56 PM	File folder
L3G4200D	4/23/2014 4:56 PM	File folder
LM73	4/23/2014 4:56 PM	File folder
MPR121	4/23/2014 4:56 PM	File folder
MPU6050	4/23/2014 4:56 PM	File folder
SSD1308	4/23/2014 4:56 PM	File folder
TCA6424A	4/23/2014 4:56 PM	File folder

3. Even though you won't need all these libraries right now, you can just copy all these to the **libraries** directory of your Galileo for future use. By the way, you'll notice that there is a duplicate of the **HMC5883L** library you installed earlier, so you can decide to merge these directories.

4. Once you have these directories installed, bring up the Galileo IDE. If the IDE is already running, you'll want to restart it so it can recognize the library. Now bring up the example program that reads the raw values of the accelerometer and gyro by selecting **Examples** | **MPU6050** | **Examples** | **MPU6050_raw**, like this:

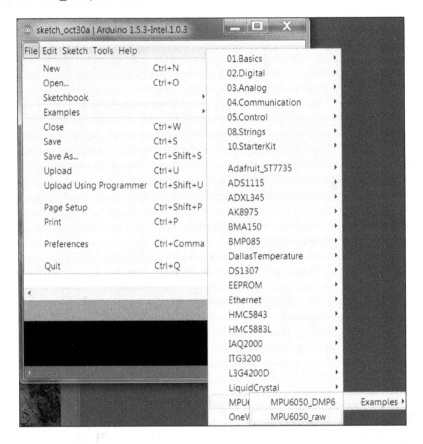

This will open a window that provides the code to read the raw data from your sensor. When you upload the code and open the Serial Monitor, you should see something like this:

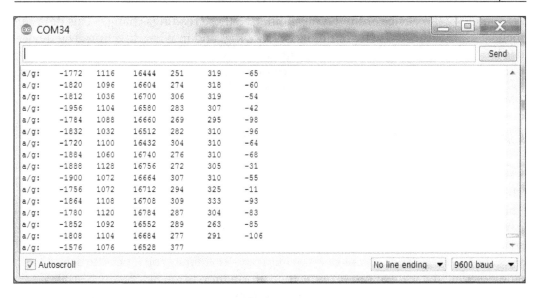

The first three numbers are the *x*, *y*, and *z* raw accelerometer readings, and the last three are *x*, *y*, and *z* angle readings from the gyroscope. If you mount the device flat in your project, *x*, *y*, and *z* would be associated with the yaw, pitch, and roll of the device. Here is a diagram of how the yaw, pitch, and roll indicate the position of a device:

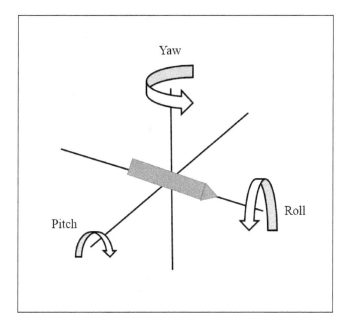

As you move the device around, you should see these readings change. This data can then be used to sense when your device is moving, and in what direction. The device has lots of capability, including the ability to set the offsets of the device so that a particular position is in the *0* position. For more information about these capabilities, feel free to look at both example programs provided by the library.

Connecting an altimeter/pressure sensor to the Galileo

The final sensor you'll learn about in this chapter is the altimeter/pressure sensor. The altimeter is useful when you want to know the altitude of your project. This is particularly useful when you want to build a robot that can fly. For more on pressure sensors and how they work, see http://www.sensorsmag.com/sensors/pressure/fundamentals-pressure-sensor-technology-846. First, you'll need to select a device. One device that can provide this information is the SainSmart **BMP085 Module, Digital Barometric Pressure Sensor**, available at many online retailers, including www.amazon.com. This device uses piezo-resistive technology to measure altitude. The following image shows this:

It looks very similar to the digital compass; just like the two previous devices, it connects via the I2C interface. You can even use the same libraries you just downloaded for the accelerometer/gyro for I2C support.

The connections between the Galileo and the device will be the same as the digital compass, like this:

Galileo Pin	Sensor Pin
5V	5V
GND	GND
A5	SCL
A4	SDA

The connections, just like those of the digital compass, are clearly marked on the back of the device, and you can use the female-to-male jumpers to make the connections.

Accessing the altimeter/pressure Sensor from the Galileo IDE

As with the previous two examples, the first step in accessing the device is to download the appropriate library. You can use the library described in the section on the accelerometer/gyro, or you can download a library just for this device. If you want to download the library for this device, go to www.sainsmart.com/ sainsmart-bmp085-digital-pressure-sensor-module-board.html page and select the **Download Link** selection towards the bottom of the **Description.** This will download a .rar file that will include an example sketch. I personally prefer to use the I2C library version, it is more up-to-date, so I will follow that example here.

Open the example by selecting **File | Examples | BMP085 | Examples | BMP085_ basic**, like this:

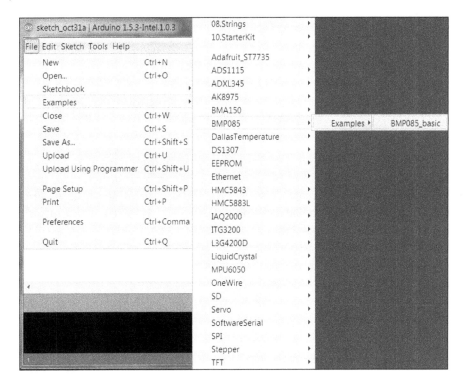

Now you can upload the sketch on the Galileo and, when you open the Serial Monitor, you should see something that looks like this:

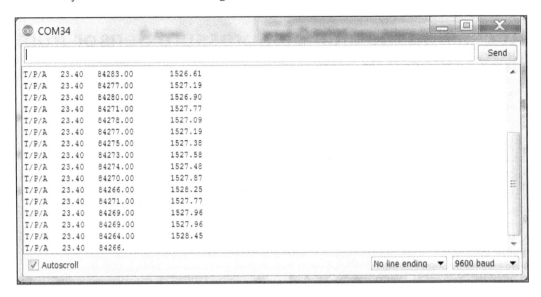

You can see not only the altitude, but the temperature and pressure as well. The *T* is the temperature in Celsius, the *P* is the pressure in Pascals, and the *A* is the altitude in meters.

Summary

There are many more sensors we could have covered in this chapter, but hopefully you have a feel for how you might be able to add them after following the instructions for these sensors. Your project now has lots of possible capabilities, but you are still tethered to the computer. In the next chapter, you'll learn how to communicate with your project wirelessly so it won't need a cable to accept commands.

6
Remote Control

Now you might want your project to be mobile. You'll at least want to disconnect it from the tether cable that you have been using to communicate with it to send control commands. In this chapter, you'll learn how to communicate wirelessly with your project. Depending on your choice of device, you'll be able to communicate across the room or across a distance of up to a mile.

In this chapter, you'll learn the following:

- How to communicate with the Galileo using an XBee transmitter/receiver, a point-to-point communication system that allows you to communicate between two Galileos or between a Galileo and a host computer

- How to configure the Galileo using a Wi-Fi mini PCI Express card so you can communicate via Wireless LAN

Connecting an XBee interface to the Galileo

One of the most popular and well-documented ways of connecting to the Galileo via an RF connection is to use an **XBee** device. This device uses a technology called **ZigBee** and it is made for longer-range wireless communications. These types of devices can work up to a range of one mile. The ZigBee standard is built upon the IEEE 802.15.4 standard, a standard that was created to allow a set of devices to communicate with each other to enable low data rate coordination of multiple devices.

The other standard that you might hear about as you try to purchase or use devices such as these is XBee. This is a specific company's implementation, Digi, of several different wireless standards with standard hardware modules that can connect in many different ways to different embedded systems. They make some that support ZigBee. Here is an image of this type of device that supports ZigBee attached to a small, XBee-specific shield that provides a USB port:

The advantage of using this device is that it is configured to make it very easy to create and manage a simple link between two XBee series #1 devices. To make this work, you'll need four items:

1. Make sure you have two XBee devices that support ZigBee series #1.

2. You'll also need to purchase a small, XBee-specific shield that provides a USB port connection to one of the two devices. This will provide communication from a host computer.

3. You'll also need to buy a shield that plugs into your Arduino so you can interface to the XBee devices. This shield is the Wireless SD card shield, and has header pins ready for the XBee device. Here is an image of the shield plugged into a Galileo, with the XBee device plugged in:

Now let's get started with configuring your two devices to talk.

Configuring the XBee devices

You'll need to configure both devices by plugging them into your host computer. Plug one of the devices into the small, XBee-specific USB shield and then connect the shield to your personal computer. Your computer should find the latest drivers for the device. If your computer does not find the device or is unable to correctly install the drivers, see `http://ftp1.digi.com/support/images/Win7DriverInstall.pdf` for help. You should see your device after you've selected **Devices and Printers** from the Start menu, like this:

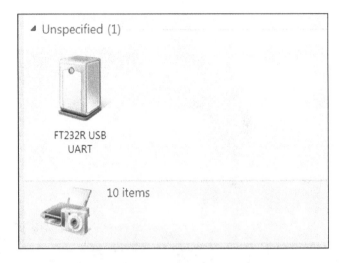

The device is now available to communicate via the IEEE 802.15.4 wireless interface. You could set up a full ZigBee-compliant network, but you're just going to communicate from one device to another directly, so you'll just use the device as a serial port connection. Double-click on the device, select the **Hardware** tab, and you should see this:

Note that the device is connected to the **COM20** serial port. You'll use this to communicate with the device and configure the device. You can use any terminal emulator program; I like to use PuTTY. If you don't have PuTTY, you can download it from www.chiark.greenend.org.uk/~sgtatham/putty/download.html. This will provide an executable that you can run to talk with and configure the devices.

Digi has recently introduced a new graphical tool for configuring XBee devices. It provides access to all the configuration settings on the XBee. If you would like to use this tool, see http://www.digi.com/products/wireless-wired-embedded-solutions/zigbee-rf-modules/xctu

Perform the following steps to configure the device:

1. Open up **PuTTY**, select **Serial,** and the (in this case) COM20 port. Here is how to fill in the PuTTY window to do this:

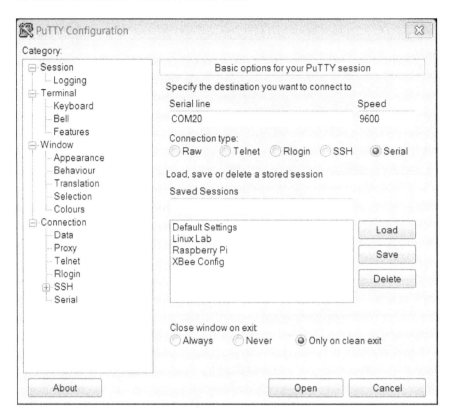

2. Configure the terminal window as shown in the screenshot:

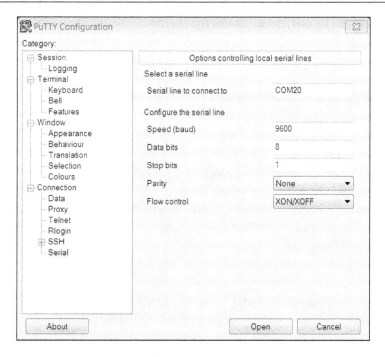

3. Now, in the **Terminal** window, make sure you also select **Local echo Force on**, and check the **Implicit CR in every LF** and **Implicit LF in every CR** (available under **Terminal** in the Category: selection.):

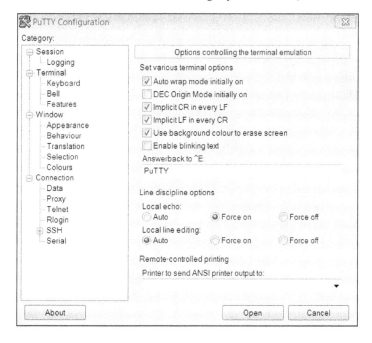

4. Connect to the device by selecting **Open**.

5. Enter the following commands by typing them into the terminal window:

The **OK** response comes back from the device as you enter each command. The first device is now configured. Remove it from the small, XBee-specific shield and plug it into the Arduino XBee shield.

Now plug the second device into the small, XBee shield and then plug it into the PC. Note that it might choose a different COM port, go to the **Devices and Printers** option, double-click on the device, and select the **Hardware** tab to find the **COM port**. Follow the same steps to configure the second device, except there are two changes. Here is the terminal window for these commands:

```
COM21 - PuTTY
+++OK
ATID3001
OK
ATMY2
OK
ATDH0
OK
ATDL1
OK
ATID
3001
ATMY
2
ATDH
0
ATDL
1
ATWR
OK
```

The two devices are now ready to communicate.

Configuring the device using a Mac is very similar. Follow these steps to start a terminal connection with the device:

1. Plug the XBee module into the XBee shield and hook it to your Mac via USB.

2. Open up a **CoolTerm** window and then hit the **Options** on the toolbar.

3. Select the correct port for your XBee device. It will look something like usbserial-XXXXXXXX.

4. If your device doesn't appear, plug it back in and click on **Re-Scan Serial Ports**.

5. Hit the **Ok** button and the rest of the defaults will work just fine.

6. Hit the **Connect** button on the toolbar and you should be talking to your XBee.

Now you can configure your device as shown previously. If you are using Linux to configure your device, you will similarly open a terminal window, connect it to the proper USB serial port, and then configure the device.

Enabling an XBee Interface in the IDE

Let's first set up the IDE for the XBee that will be connected to the Galileo. Once you have connected the shield to the Galileo, simply connect the Galileo with the USB cable to your host computers. Bring up the IDE and then type in the following code into the sketch window:

```
XbeeExample | Arduino 1.5.3-Intel.1.0.3

File  Edit  Sketch  Tools  Help

XbeeExample §

TTYUARTClass* gSerialStdPtr = &Serial; // Galileo, /dev/ttyGS0, Tx pin
TTYUARTClass* gSerialTwoPtr = &Serial1; // Galileo, /dev/ttyS0, Rx pin
bool gGalileo = true;
bool qData;
void setup()
{
  qData = false; // Initialize on reset
  gSerialStdPtr->begin(9600); // Receiver
  gSerialTwoPtr->begin(9600); // Sender
  waitForUser(5); // Give user time to open serial terminal
  gSerialStdPtr->println("XBee-Receiver-setup");
}
void loop()
{
// Give indication that no data has been received
  if(qData == false)
    gSerialStdPtr->println("XBee-Receiver-waiting");
// Get data from Sender and print to Receiver serial port
  while(gSerialTwoPtr->available())
  {
    char c= gSerialTwoPtr->read();// Read XBee data
    gSerialStdPtr->write(c); // Write local
    qData = true;
  }
  if(qData == false) delay(1000*1); // Slow down until data is rec
}

void waitForUser(unsigned int aSec)
{
// Give user time to bring up the serial port
  for(int i=aSec; i>0; i--)
  {
    delay(1000*1);
    gSerialStdPtr->print(i);
  }
  gSerialStdPtr->println("");
}

Done uploading.
Transfer complete

22                                              Intel® Galileo on COM40
```

Here is an explanation of this set of code:

- This set of code initializes the serial port on the Galileo, so you can receive via the serial interface:

```
TTYUARTClass* gSerialStdPtr = &Serial; // Galileo, /dev/ttyGS0, Tx
pin
TTYUARTClass* gSerialTwoPtr = &Serial1; // Galileo, /dev/ttyS0, Rx
pin
bool gGalileo = true;
bool qData;
int led = 13;
```

- This set of code starts the send and receive process, you'll only use the receive process for this application:

```
qData = false; // Initialize on reset
gSerialStdPtr->begin(9600); // Receiver
gSerialTwoPtr->begin(9600); // Sender
waitForUser(5); // Give usr time to open serial terminal
gSerialStdPtr->println("XBee-Receiver-setup");
pinMode(led, OUTPUT);
```

- This code waits for a valid input from the serial port on the Xbee and then prints it to the Serial Monitor screen. It also takes the data and turns on the onboard LED, connected to Pin 13, if the input is a *1*; it turns it off if the data is a *0*:

```
  if(qData == false)
    gSerialStdPtr->println("XBee-Receiver-waiting");
//Get data from Sender and print to Receiver serial port
  while(gSerialTwoPtr->available())
  {
    char c= gSerialTwoPtr->read();// Read XBee data
  if (c == '1')
    digitalWrite(led, HIGH);
  if (c == '0')
    digitalWrite(led, LOW);
    gSerialStdPtr->write(c); // Write local
    qData = true;
  }
  if(qData == false) delay(1000*1); // Slow down until
      data is rec
}
```

- This code waits for a set time for the user to bring up the serial port:

```
void waitForUser(unsigned int aSec)
{
// Give user time to bring up the serial port
  for(int i=aSec; i>0; i--)
  {
    delay(1000*1);
    gSerialStdPtr->print(i);
  }
  gSerialStdPtr->println("");
}
```

Once the code is uploaded, you'll need to physically change a switch setting on the Wireless Shield, so the device will now accept commands from your XBee controller. It is on the opposite end of the shield from the device, and looks like this:

This switch connects the XBee to either the USB serial port or the microcontroller (in this case, the Galileo) serial port. Change it to the MICRO setting once your sketch has finished compilation and uploaded to the Galileo.

Now connect the other XBee device via the small, Xbee-specific USB shield to the computer. Open **PuTTY** or an other terminal emulator window. Make sure you set the terminal emulator data rate to 9600 baud. In PuTTY, your configuration will look like this:

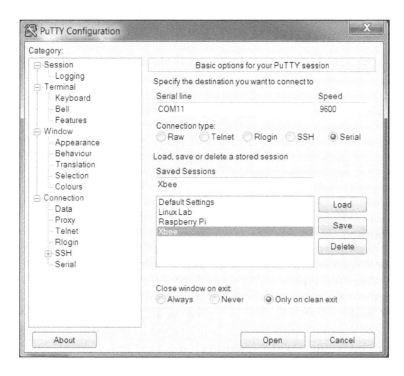

Now open the terminal window. You should now be able to enter commands into the Putty window and monitor them using the Serial Monitor on the Galileo. Here is a picture of the Putty application:

Here is what you should see if you open the Serial Monitor on your Galileo:

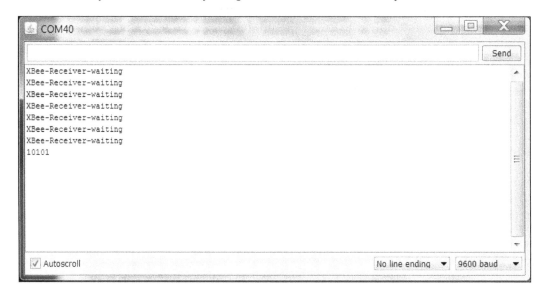

Most importantly, each time you enter a *1* you should see the LED on the Galileo turn on and, when you type a *0*, you should see it turn off. Now, if your system is not working, there are a couple of ways to try and determine what is going wrong. First and foremost, make sure the Galileo is turned on and is executing the correct code. Second, check to see that characters are being typed in the Putty window. Third, check the baud rate of the PuTTY window. If it is too high, you will see characters come through the system, but you they will not be interpreted correctly on the Galileo. Fourth, make sure you actually configured both the devices instead of just one. Fifth, make sure the serial switch on the Xbee shield is in the right position. Finally, make sure the devices are in range.

Configuring a Wi-Fi connection on the Galileo

You can also communicate with the Galileo via Wireless LAN. To do this, you'll need some additional hardware. The first piece of hardware you'll need is a mini PCI wireless device. The basic Galileo Poky operating system supports two devices: the **Intel® Centrino® Wireless-N 135** and **Intel® Centrino® Advanced-N 6205** adapters. If you don't want to compile your own drivers, you should purchase one of these two devices.

If you wish to purchase a different mini PCI wireless device, see `http://www.malinov.com/Home/sergey-s-blog/intelgalileo-addingwifi` for how to compile drivers for your device.

You'll also need some cables and antennas. You'll need two 6dBi RPSMA antennas and two 8-inch UFL cables. There are kits available, for example at `http://www.amazon.com/gp/product/B00DP64JRG`. Also useful is a Half to Full Height Mini **PCI Express (PCI-E)** Card Bracket Adapter, this makes the wireless card easier to install. Once you've gathered all the hardware, install the card into the Galileo. It is straightforward but, if you get confused, follow the instructions at `http://ionospherics.com/intel-galileo-setting-up-wifi/` to install all the hardware into the Galileo. Here is what it should look like:

Once you have the wireless hardware setup, you'll also need a cable to establish a terminal connection to the Linux operating system on your device. For the Intel Galileo Gen2 board, the cable you will need is a USB connector on one end and a FDTI 6 pin connector on the other. These are available at most online electronics stores:

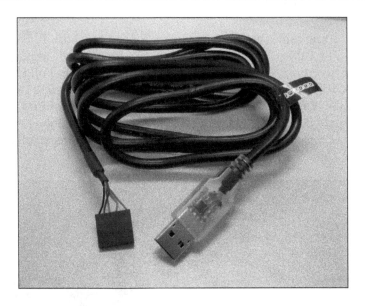

If you are using the Galileo Gen1 board, this is 3.5mm to USB cable. Plug this cable into the terminal port on the Galileo, and the USB connector on your host computer.

Now that you have all the hardware, here are the steps to get your Galileo up and connected to Wi-Fi:

1. First, you'll need a new version of the Linux operating system for your Galileo. To get this go to `http://www.intel.com/content/www/us/en/do-it-yourself/downloads-and-documentation.html#galileo` software and select **Download SD-Card Linux Image for Intel Galileo (48 MB, .bz2)**. This will download a `.tar` file (an archived file) with the support for your wireless connection.

2. You'll need to un-archive this file using an archive utility such as 7-Zip.

3. Now copy all the files under the **SDCard** directory onto a micro SD card.

4. You'll need a terminal window to interact with your Galileo. If you are using Windows, you'll need a terminal emulator window to communicate with the Galileo. One popular, free version is called Putty. For more information on Putty and how to download, see `http://www.chiark.greenend.org.uk/~sgtatham/putty/`. However, any terminal emulator program will do. Both Linux and the Apple OS come with terminal emulator programs.

5. Open a terminal window and select the serial port that is connected to the USB to the FTDI connector using a baud rate of 115200. Every time the Galileo boots, it will look for an image on the SD card and boot that image if it is present. If it is not present, it will boot the Poky version that is in the internal memory. The terminal window will allow you to select between the two. You'll now want to boot the unit using the micro SD card and the new version of the Galileo operating system by installing the card and applying power. You should see this boot up screen:

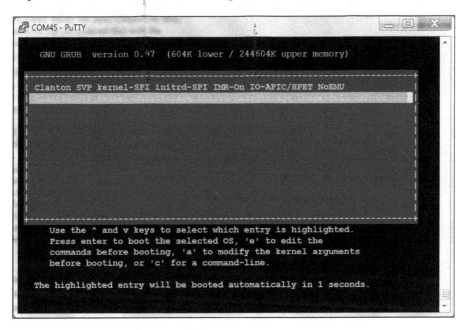

If not already highlighted, select the second choice here to boot from the card.

6. Now log in to the system using root as the user.

7. Type ifconfig -a. This should show all LAN interfaces, and should look like this:

```
COM45 - PuTTY
clanton login: root
root@clanton:~# ifconfig -a
eth0      Link encap:Ethernet  HWaddr 98:4F:EE:01:9B:2B
          UP BROADCAST MULTICAST  MTU:1500  Metric:1
          RX packets:0 errors:0 dropped:0 overruns:0 frame:0
          TX packets:1 errors:0 dropped:0 overruns:0 carrier:0
          collisions:0 txqueuelen:1000
          RX bytes:0 (0.0 B)  TX bytes:322 (322.0 B)
          Interrupt:40 Base address:0x8000

lo        Link encap:Local Loopback
          inet addr:127.0.0.1  Mask:255.0.0.0
          inet6 addr: ::1/128 Scope:Host
          UP LOOPBACK RUNNING  MTU:65536  Metric:1
          RX packets:0 errors:0 dropped:0 overruns:0 frame:0
          TX packets:0 errors:0 dropped:0 overruns:0 carrier:0
          collisions:0 txqueuelen:0
          RX bytes:0 (0.0 B)  TX bytes:0 (0.0 B)

wlan0     Link encap:Ethernet  HWaddr 08:11:96:38:02:38
          BROADCAST MULTICAST  MTU:1500  Metric:1
          RX packets:0 errors:0 dropped:0 overruns:0 frame:0
          TX packets:0 errors:0 dropped:0 overruns:0 carrier:0
          collisions:0 txqueuelen:1000
          RX bytes:0 (0.0 B)  TX bytes:0 (0.0 B)
```

You can see the wlan0 interface that is now available to connect to your Wi-Fi network. However, there is no address assigned; as you can see, there is no inet addr: line in the wlan0 section. You can use the IDE to connect to your network, this will be shown in the next section.

If you want to auto connect to a given network each time you boot the Galileo, you'll need to add your wireless network ID and password to the wpa_supplicant. conf file. To do this, type wpa_passphrase WIFI-SSID WIFI-PASSPHRASE> /etc/wpa_supplicant.conf.

8. You will need to edit one more file to ensure access to the Wi-Fi connection each time you boot your Galileo. The file is /etc/networks/config. Edit this file using vi (vi is the editor that comes on this Linux release.) Add auto wlan0 as the last line.

9. Reboot your system, as before. Log-in using root as the user.

Now that the hardware is connected, you can access the wireless capabilities inside the IDE.

Using Wi-Fi from the IDE

Now that the hardware is up-and-running, you can run the examples in the IDE.
If you bring up the IDE and select **Examples | Wi-Fi**, you can see that there are
many choices:

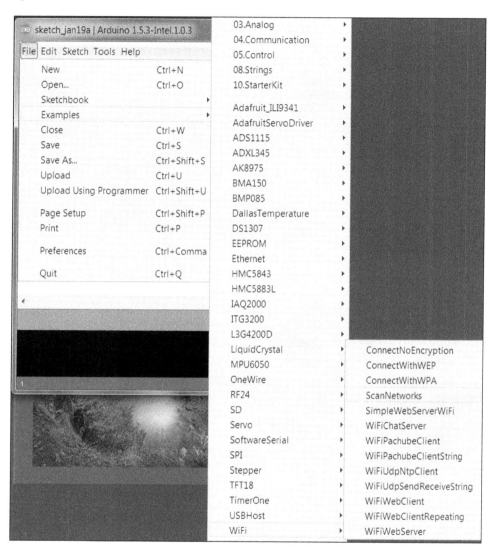

The most basic of these choices is the **ScanNetworks** sketch. If you select this sketch and then open the Serial Monitor Window, you should see something like this:

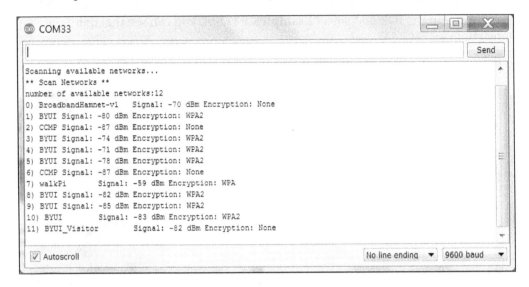

The other sketches provide further capabilities. There are sketches that show how to connect using WPA or WEP security protocols. One of the most useful is the SimpleWebServer Wi-Fi that shows how to turn an LED on and off over the Wi-Fi network via an external web page. Simply connect a resistor and LED in series between GND and digital IO pin nine, edit the sketch to include the SSID and password of your network, and then open a web browser. When you open the Serial Monitor, it will show you connected to the network:

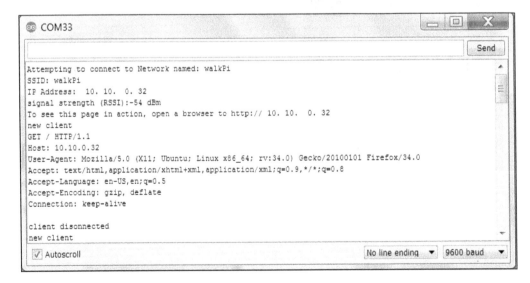

Now go on the host computer and enter the address shown in the address line. The following should appear on your browser:

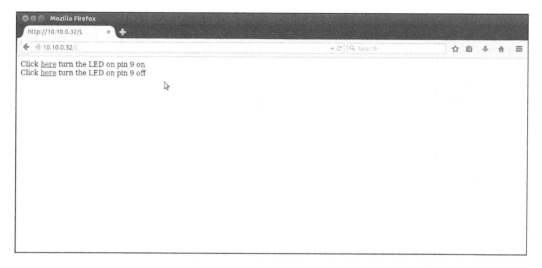

You can now turn the LED on and off.

Summary

As you now know, there are several useful ways of connecting wirelessly with your Arduino. In this chapter, you've learned how to connect your project wirelessly using XBee, a reliable long-range interface. You've also learned how to connect via Wi-Fi. Now your project can go untethered, needing only an occasional battery charge to keep it up-and-running. In the next chapter, you'll learn how to access the Linux system on Galileo and access even more interesting capabilities.

7
Going Further with Galileo

With your Galileo, you've learned how to build projects that can roll, now let's build one that can walk. In this final chapter, you'll move from using the simple Galileo IDE to using the Linux capabilities of the Galileo to drive an external USB servo controller so that you can control the 12 servos that will make your quadruped move.

In this chapter, you will learn how to use the Galileo's Linux capabilities to control a basic quadruped platform. To do this you will learn the following:

- Galileo's Linux capabilities
- How servos work
- How to use the Galileo's Linux capabilities to control a servo controller that can control lots of servos
- Creating complex movements out of simple servo commands

The Galileo and Linux

While you have been accessing the Galileo exclusively through the IDE, the Galileo actually has been running a version of the Linux operating system all along. Linux is an operating system similar to Windows, or the Apple Mac operating system. In fact, the Mac operating system is built upon a version of Unix, which is very similar to Linux. Now Linux, unlike Windows, Android, or IOS, is not tightly controlled by a single company. It is a group effort, mostly open source, and while it is available for free, it grows and develops based on community development and support.

Thus, a number of distributions have emerged, each built on a similar kernel, or core set of capabilities. These core capabilities are all based on the Linux specification. However, they are packaged slightly differently, and developed, supported, and packaged by different organizations. Angstrom is one of these versions. Debian is another. There are others as well. The one included in the internal memory associated with the Galileo is called Poky, and is built using a set of tools called **Yocto**. Yocto is a toolkit that allows users to build their own Linux distribution.

For this project, you're going to create a new SD card image of Linux with a Debian distribution, install it on a microSD card, and boot the Galileo from the card. This is a very popular version of Linux that supports a wide range of different capabilities.

Now you'll need to connect the Galileo to the LAN to add capability. There are two ways to do this. The first is using a wired connection; you can simply connect the Galileo directly by connecting a LAN cable to the connector on the Galileo. You can also connect the Galileo using a Wi-Fi connection. This requires you to add additional Hardware and configure your Wi-Fi connection. See `https://software.intel.com/en-us/blogs/2014/03/13/configuring-wifi-for-the-intel-galileo-board` or `http://www.hackshed.co.uk/how-to-use-wifi-with-the-intel-galileo` for more information on how to assemble, configure, and connect your Galileo to a Wi-Fi network.

Creating and booting the Debian Linux SD card image on the Galileo

Here are the steps to follow to install and run the Debian image on your Galileo:

1. The first thing you'll need is a Debian Linux image that supports LAN and DHCP. The site at `https://communities.intel.com/message/231688` has a version, there are others. If you go to this site, you can download this file.

2. If you are using Windows on your computer, this file will now exist in your **Downloads** directory. Unzip this file and you should end up with a **galileo.img** file.

3. Now you need a program that will write this file to a micro SD card. If you are using Windows, download the program **Win32DiskImager** from `http://sourceforge.net/projects/win32diskimager/`. Install this program on your PC. If you are using Linux, you can use the dd command to write to the card.

4. If you are using a PC, run **Win32DiskImager**. Insert your microSD card into your PC. You might need a microSD to USB adapter for this. Now, specify the file and the card in **Win32DiskImager**, like this:

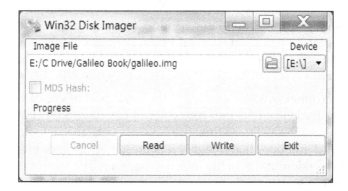

Be careful in selecting the device, you can corrupt a drive if you choose the wrong one. If you are using Linux, use the command `sudo dd if=galileo.img of=sdX` where the `sdX` is the location of the card you want to write to.

5. Now take the card and insert it into the Galileo's microSD slot.

6. To monitor your system, you will want to connect a terminal cable between the Galileo and your host computer. If you are using the Galileo Gen2 board, the cable you will want will have a USB connector on one end and a FDTI 6 pin connector on the other. These are available at most online electronics stores:

If you are using the Galileo Gen1 board, this is a 3.5 mm to USB cable.

7. You'll now want to boot the unit using the microSD card and Debian by applying power, but first also connect the LAN cable and serial cable. For the Galileo Gen2, the serial cable connects right next to the LAN connector; there is a 6 pin FTDI connector for the cable.

8. You'll need a terminal emulator window to communicate with the Galileo. One popular, free version is called Putty. For more information on Putty and how to download, see http://www.chiark.greenend.org.uk/~sgtatham/putty/. However, any terminal emulator program will do.

9. Open a terminal window and select the serial port of your USB to FTDI connector (or USB-to-3.5 mm connector, if you have a GEN 1 board) and a baud rate of 115200. Every time the Galileo boots, it will look for an image on the SD card and boot that image if it is present. If it is not present, it will boot the Poky version that is in the internal memory. The terminal emulator will allow you to select which operating system you want to run.

10. Power on the unit. You should see this boot up screen:

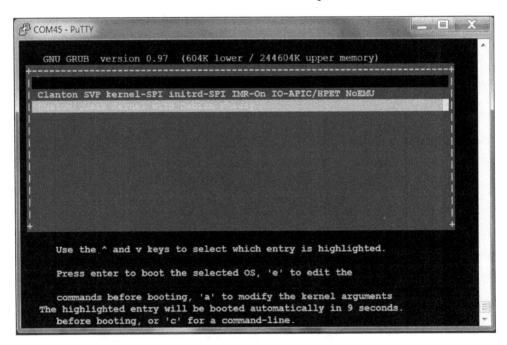

11. Select the last selection on this list. The unit will now boot from the Debian Linux distribution on the card. Type the username and password, for this distribution it is user and user. The unit will now provide a terminal connection from your host computer where you can type commands.

12. You will need to edit a file to get access to the LAN connection. The file is /etc/networks/config. Edit this file using either vi, or nano (both are editors that come with this Linux release.) Make sure the file looks like this:

```
user@Galileo:~$ cat /etc/network/interfaces

# interfaces(5) file used by ifup(8) and ifdown(8)

auto lo

auto eth0

iface eth0 inet dhcp

user@Galileo:~$
```

13. Reboot your system.

14. Run the command sudo ifconfig. and you should be able to see the IP address of your Galileo.

15. This image is quite small. When you write the image to your card, the system will now see your SD card as quite small as well, even if you have a much larger card with more memory available. You can follow the instructions at http://sourceforge.net/p/galileodebian/wiki/How%20to%20 expand%20the%20root%20filesystem%20to%20use%20the%20entire%20 SD%20card/ to expand your card to its full size.

Now your system is up and running and connected to the Internet. This particular distribution also has python available, which you will use later. You will want to run the command sudo apt-get update to update the links for any installs you want to do in the future. You will also want to run the command sudo apt-get upgrade to update your system to the latest.

Building robots that can walk

Now that your Galileo can run Linux, you'll need to build a quadruped that has four legs. You'll be using 12 servos so each leg has three points that can move, or three **degrees of freedom (DOF)**. You could use the IDE and its General Purpose Input/Output (GPIO) pins to control a limited number of servos. However, you need to control 12 servos for this project, so this won't work. In this project, you'll use an external servo controller that can supply the control signals and voltages for all 12 servos. This example will also show you how to use the Linux capabilities of the Galileo for even more complex robotics projects.

Since servos are the main component of this project, it is perhaps useful to go through a tutorial on servos and how to control them.

How servo motors work

Servo motors are somewhat similar to DC motors; however, there is an important difference. While DC motors are generally designed to move in a continuous way — rotating 360 degrees at a given speed — servos are generally designed to move to a limited set of angles. In other words, in the DC motor world, you generally want your motors to spin with a continuous rotation speed that you control. In the servo world, you want your motor to move to a specific position that you control.

This is done by sending a **Pulse-Width-Modulated (PWM)** signal on the control connector of the servo. The length of this pulse will control the angle of the servo, like this:

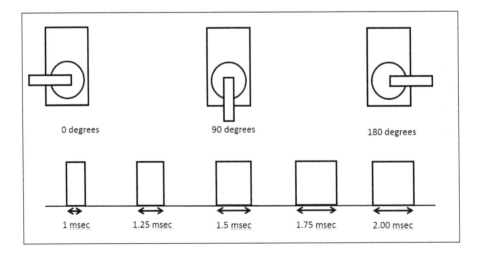

These pulses are sent out with a repetition rate of 60 Hz. You can position the servo to any angle by setting the correct control pulse.

Building the quadruped platform

You'll first need some parts so you can build your quadruped robot. There are several kits out there, including the ones found at `www.trossenrobotics.com/p/PhantomX-AX-12-Quadruped.aspx`. However, such kits can be expensive so, for this example, you'll create your own kit using a set of Lynxmotion parts. These are available from several online retailers, such as `www.robotshop.com`. To build this quadruped, you'll need two sets each of the two leg parts, and then one set each of the body. Here are the parts with their robotshop part number:

Quantity	Description
1	Lynxmotion Symmetric Quadrapod Body Kit - Mini QBK-02
2	Lynxmotion 3" Aluminum Femur Pair
2	Lynxmotion Robot Leg "A" Pair (No Servo) RL-01
4	Lynxmotion Aluminum Multi-Purpose Servo Bracket Two Pack ASB-04
2	Ball Bearing with Flange - 3mm ID (pair) Product Code : RB-Lyn-317

The last part is not a Lynxmotion part, but is a bearing you'll need to connect the leg to the body.

You'll also need 12 standard size servos. There are several possible choices, but I personally like the Hitec servos. They are a very inexpensive servo you can get at most hobby shops and online electronics retailers. Now let's talk briefly about the model of servo. Servos come in different model numbers, primarily based on the amount of torque they can generate.

Torque is the force that the servo can exert to move the part connected to it. In this case, your servos will need to lift and move the weight associated with your quadruped, so you'll need a servo with enough torque to do this. In this case, I suggest you use eight model **HS-485HB** servos, you'll use these for the servos attached to the end of the leg and for the body. Then you'll use four model **HS-645MG** servos for the middle of the leg; this is the servo that will require the highest amount of torque. You can also just use twelve HS-645MG servos, but they are more expensive than the HS-485, so using the two different servos will be less expensive.

Here are the steps for assembling the quadruped:

1. Put the lower part of the right leg together; it should look like this:

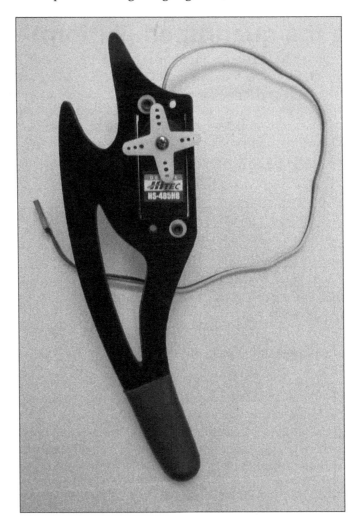

2. Now connect this assembly to an interconnecting piece, like this:

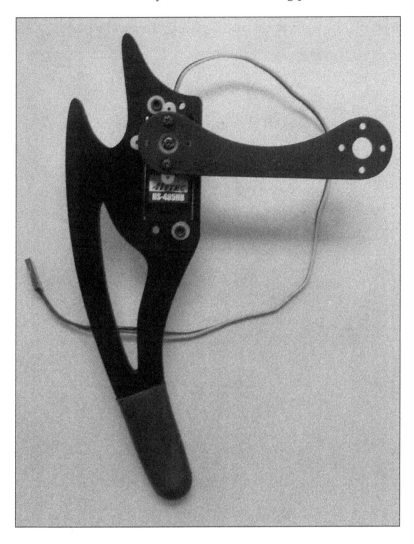

3. Complete the leg by connecting two of the servo brackets together at right angles, mounting the HS-645MG onto one of the brackets and then connecting this servo to the interconnected piece, like this:

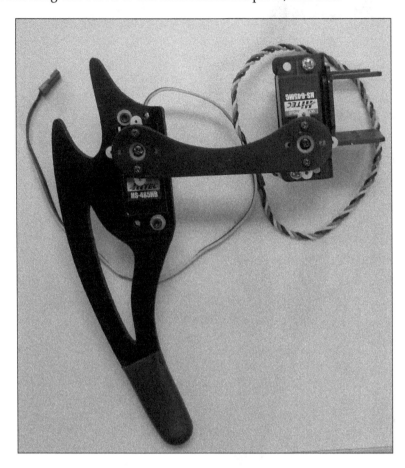

4. Put another right leg together.

5. Now put two left legs together following the same steps as mentioned previously, but in left leg configuration. They look like this:

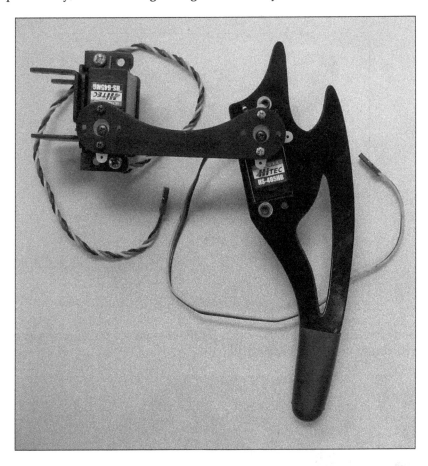

6. The next step is to build the body kit. There are some instructions at
    www.lynxmotion.com/images/html/sq3u-assembly.htm, but it
    should look like this:

7. Then connect each leg to the body kit. First, connect the empty servo bracket
    to the body using the bearing, like this:

8. Now connect the other servo to the empty servo bracket and the body, like this:

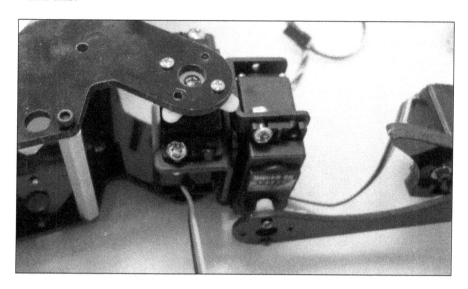

Your quadruped should now look like this:

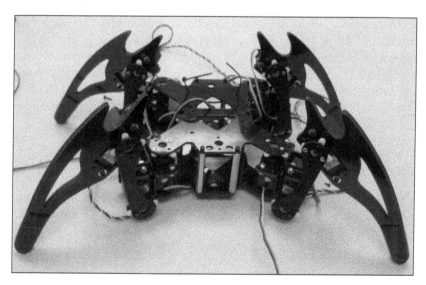

Now that you have the basic hardware assembled, you can turn your attention to the electronics.

Using a servo controller to control the servos

To make your quadruped walk, you first need to connect the servo motor controller to the servos.The servo controller you are going to use for this project is a simple servo motor controller utilizing USB from Pololu (Pololu item #: 1354 available at www.pololu.com) that can control 18 servo motors. Here is an image of the unit:

Make sure you order the assembled version. This piece of hardware will turn USB commands from the Galileo into signals that control your servo motors. Pololu makes a number of different versions of this controller, each able to control a certain number of servos. In this case, you might want to choose the 18 servo version so you can control all 12 servos with one controller and also add an additional servo to control the direction of a camera or sensor. You could also choose the 12-servo version. One advantage of the 18-servo controller is the ease of connecting power to the unit via screw type connectors.

There are two connections you'll need to make to the servo controller to get started; the first to the servo motors, and the second to a battery.

First, connect the servos to the controller. In order to be consistent, let's connect your 12 servos to the connections marked zero through 11 on the controller using this configuration:

Servo Connector	Servo
0	Right Front Lower Leg
1	Right Front Middle Leg
2	Right Front Upper Leg
3	Right Rear Lower Leg

Servo Connector	Servo
4	Right Rear Middle Leg
5	Right Rear Upper Leg
6	Left Front Lower Leg
7	Left Front Middle Leg
8	Left Front Upper Leg
9	Left Rear Lower Leg
10	Left Rear Middle Leg
11	Left Rear Upper Leg

Here is a picture of the back of the controller; this will tell us where to connect our servos:

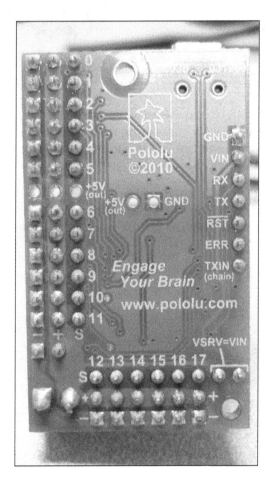

Now you need to connect the servo motor controller to your battery. For this project, you can use a 2S RC LiPo battery, it will supply the 7.4 volts and the current needed by your servos, which can be in the order of 2 Amps. Here is a picture:

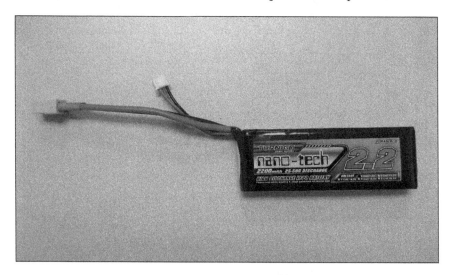

This battery will come with two connectors, one with larger-gauge wires for normal usage and a smaller connector for connecting to the battery recharger. You can use the XT60 Connector Pairs, solder some wires to the mating connector of the battery, and then insert the bare end of the wires into the servo controller.

Your system is now functional. Now you'll connect the motor controller to your personal computer to check to see if you can communicate with it. To do this, connect a mini USB cable between the servo controller and your personal computer.

Communicating with the servo controller via a PC

Now that the hardware is connected, you can use some software provided by Polulu to control the servos. Let's do this by using your personal computer. First, download the Polulu software from `www.pololu.com/docs/0J40/3.a` and install it based on the instructions on the website. Once it is installed, run the software and you should see this screen:

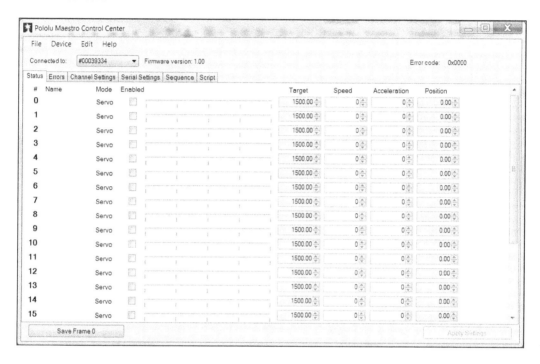

You will first need to change the configuration on Serial Settings, so select the Serial Settings tabs and you should see this:

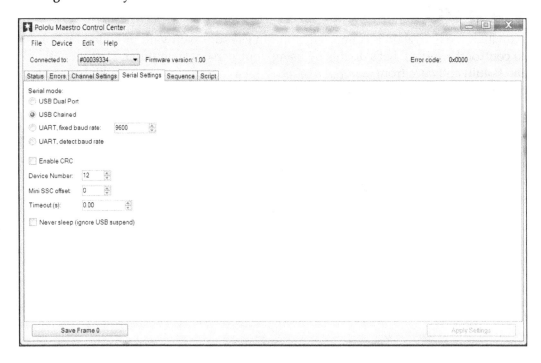

Make sure that the USB Chained option is selected, this will allow you to connect and control the motor controller over USB. Now go back to the main screen by selecting the Status tab and now you can actually turn on the twelve servos. The screen should look like this:

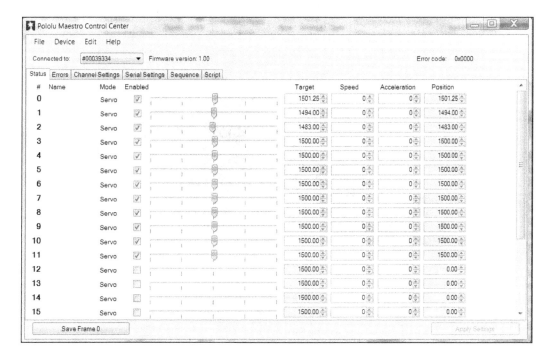

Now you can use the sliders to actually control the servos. Make sure that the servo 0 moves the right front lower servo, 1 the right front middle servo, 2 the right front upper servo, and so on. You can also use this to center the servos. Set all the servos so that the slider is in the middle. Now, unscrew the servo horn on each servo until the servos are centered at this location. At the zero location of all servos, your quadruped should look like this:

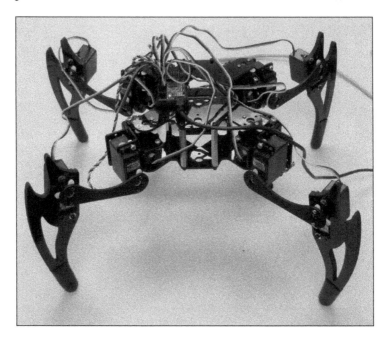

Connecting the servo controller to the Galileo

You've checked the servo motor controller and the servos; you'll now connect the motor controller up to the Galileo and make sure you can control the servos from it.

Let's now talk to the motor controller. Here are the steps:

1. Connect Galileo to the motor controller by connecting a mini USB-to-mini USB cable. Connect the cable to the USB host connection on the Galileo, like this:

2. Download the Linux code from Pololu at `www.pololu.com/docs/0J40/3.b.` Perhaps the best way is to log onto your Galileo, then type wget `http://www.pololu.com/file/download/maestro-linux-100507.tar.gz?file_id=0J315`.

3. Then, move the file using this command:

```
mv maestro-linux-100507.tar.gz\?file_id\=0J315 maestro-
linux-100507.tar.gz
```

4. Unpack the file by typing `tar -xzfv maestro_linux_011507.tar.gz`. This will create a directory called `maestro_linux`. Go to that directory by typing `cd maestro_linux` and then type `ls`, you should see something like this:

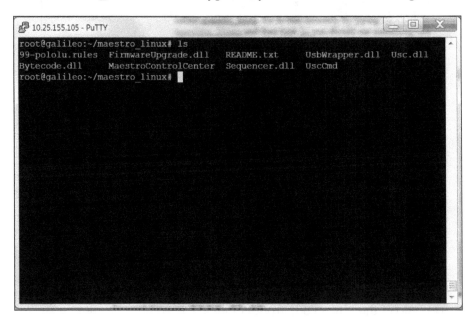

The document `README.txt` will give you explicit instructions on how to install the software. Unfortunately, you can't run **MaestroControlCenter** on your Galileo, your version of windows doesn't support the graphics, but you can control your servos using the **UscCmd** command line application. First type `./UscCmd --list` and you should see the following:

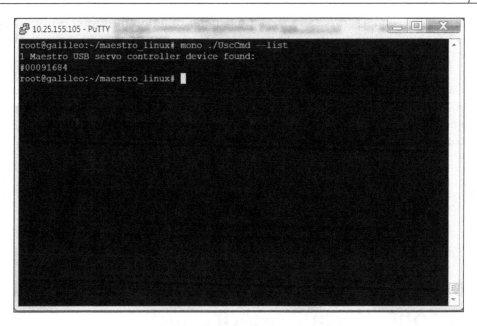

The unit sees your servo controller. If you just type mono ./UscCmd, you can see all the commands you can send to your controller:

Notice you can send a servo a specific target angle, although the target is not in angle values so it makes it a bit difficult to know where you are sending your servo. With a servo and battery connected to the servo controller, try typing ./UscCmd --servo 0, 10. The servo will move to its full angle position. Type ./UscCmd - servo 0, 0 and it will stop the servo from trying to move. In the next section, you'll write some python code that will translate your angles to the commands that the servo controller will want to see to move it to specific angle locations. If you are struggling with the USB connection, see http://www.linux-usb.org/FAQ.html for more information.

 If you didn't run the Windows version of Maestro Controller and set the **Serial Settings** to **USB Chained,** your motor controller might not respond. Rerun the Maestro Controller code and set the **Serial Settings** to **USB Chained**.

Creating a program in Linux so that you can control your quadruped

You now know that you can talk to your servo motor controller, and move your servos. In this section, you'll create a python program that will let you talk to your servos to move them to specific angles. You'll use python as it is very simple and easy to run.

Let's start with a simple program that will make your legged mobile robot's servos go to 90 degrees (this should be somewhere close to the middle of the 0 to 180 degrees you can set.) If you are unfamiliar with the editing code in Linux, the best source is a tutorial on the editor you are using. For nano try http://www.howtogeek.com/howto/42980/the-beginners-guide-to-nano-the-linux-command-line-text-editor/. Here is the code:

```
10.25.155.105 - PuTTY                                    _ □ X
File Edit Options Buffers Tools Python Help
#!/usr/bin/python
import serial
import time

def setAngle(ser, channel, angle):
    minAngle = 0.0
    maxAngle = 180.0
    minTarget = 256.0
    maxTarget = 13120.0
    scaledValue = int((angle / ((maxAngle - minAngle) / (maxTarget - minTarget)\
)) + minTarget)
    commandByte = chr(0x84)
    channelByte = chr(channel)
    lowTargetByte = chr(scaledValue & 0x7F)
    highTargetByte = chr((scaledValue >> 7) & 0x7F)
    command = commandByte + channelByte + lowTargetByte + highTargetByte
    ser.write(command)
    ser.flush()

ser = serial.Serial("/dev/ttyACM0", 9600)

# Home position
for i in range(0, 15):
    setAngle(ser, i, 90)

ser.close()

-11-:----F1   quad.py         All L1      (Python)-------------------------------
For information about GNU Emacs and the GNU system, type C-h C-a.
```

Here is an explanation of the code:

1. `#!/usr/bin/python:`- This first line allows you to make this python file execute from the command line.

2. `import serial:`- This line imports the serial library. You need the serial library to talk to your unit via USB.

3. `def setAngle(ser, channel, angle):`- This function converts your desired setting of servo and angle into the serial command that the servo motor controller needs. To understand the specifics of the code used to control the servos, see `https://www.pololu.com/docs/0J40`.

4. `ser = serial.Serial("/dev/ttyACM0", 9600): `- This opens the serial port connection to your servo controller.

5. Now you can set each servo to the middle (home) position:

```
for i in range(0, 15):
setAngle(ser, i, 90)
```

The default would be to set each servo to 90 degrees. If your legs aren't in their middle position, you can adjust them by adjusting the position of the servo horns on each servo.

To access the serial port, you'll need to make sure you have the python serial library. If you don't, then type `apt-get install python-serial`. After you have installed the serial library, you can run your program by typing `python quad.py`.

Once you have the basic home position set, you can now ask your robot to do some things. Let's start by having your quadruped wave. Here is the python code:

```
10.25.155.105 - PuTTY

File Edit Options Buffers Tools Python Help
#!/usr/bin/python
import serial
import time

def setAngle(ser, channel, angle):
    minAngle = 0.0
    maxAngle = 180.0
    minTarget = 256.0
    maxTarget = 13120.0
    scaledValue = int((angle / ((maxAngle - minAngle) / (maxTarget - minTarget)\
)) + minTarget)
    commandByte = chr(0x84)
    channelByte = chr(channel)
    lowTargetByte = chr(scaledValue & 0x7F)
    highTargetByte = chr((scaledValue >> 7) & 0x7F)
    command = commandByte + channelByte + lowTargetByte + highTargetByte
    ser.write(command)
    ser.flush()

ser = serial.Serial("/dev/ttyACM0", 9600)

# Home position
for i in range(0, 15):
    setAngle(ser, i, 90)

setAngle(ser, 1, 100)
time.sleep(1)
setAngle(ser, 0, 130)
time.sleep(1)
setAngle(ser, 0, 100)
time.sleep(1)
setAngle(ser, 0, 130)
time.sleep(1)
setAngle(ser, 0, 100)
time.sleep(1)
setAngle(ser, 0, 90)
time.sleep(1)
setAngle(ser, 1, 90)
ser.close()

-11-:----F1   quad.py        All L1      (Python)-------------------------------
For information about GNU Emacs and the GNU system, type C-h C-a.
```

In this case, you are using your `setAngle` command to set your servos to manipulate your robot's front right arm. The middle servo raises the arm, and the lower survey then goes back and forth between an angle of *100* and *130*.

One of the most basic actions you'll want your robot to take is to walk forward. Here is an example of how to manipulate the legs to make this happen:

```
# Home position
for i in range(0, 15):
    setAngle(ser, i, 90)

setAngle(ser, 4, 110)
time.sleep(1)
setAngle(ser, 5, 100)
time.sleep(1)
setAngle(ser, 4, 90)
time.sleep(1)
setAngle(ser, 7, 70)
time.sleep(1)
setAngle(ser, 8, 80)
time.sleep(1)
setAngle(ser, 7, 90)
time.sleep(1)
setAngle(ser, 1, 110)
time.sleep(1)
setAngle(ser, 2, 100)
time.sleep(1)
setAngle(ser, 1, 90)
time.sleep(1)
setAngle(ser, 10, 70)
time.sleep(1)
setAngle(ser, 11, 80)
time.sleep(1)
setAngle(ser, 10, 90)

for i in range(0, 15):
    setAngle(ser, i, 90)


ser.close()
```

```
-11-:**--F1   quad.py          Bot L52      (Python)-------------------------
```

This program lifts and then moves forward each leg, one at a time, then moves all the legs to the home position, which moves the robot forward. Not the most elegant, but it does work. There are more sophisticated algorithms for walking with your quadruped, see `http://letsmakerobots.com/node/35354` and `https://www.youtube.com/watch?v=jWP3RnYa_tw`. Once you have the program working, you'll want to package all your hardware onto the mobile robot.

You can make your robot do many amazing things. Walk forward, walk backward, dance, turn around; any number of movements are possible. The best way to learn is to try new and different positions with the servos.

Summary

You now have a robot than can walk! This should now give you the opportunity to use the Linux system to add more complex capabilities. Debian is quite powerful, and opens an entire set of open-source capabilities. In the next chapter, you'll explore using the Galileo to produce speech.

8

Speech Output

Now that you've learned how to get to the Linux operating system on your Galileo, you have a whole new set of capabilities that you can add to your projects. One example is speech; it is a good basic project and offers an example of adding capability in both hardware and software. You'll be adding a speaker to your Galileo. You'll also add functionality so the robot can respond via the speaker.

Specifically, in this chapter you'll learn how to:

- Hook up the hardware to input sound
- Use Espeak to allow your projects to respond in a robot voice

This project requires a USB microphone or speaker adapter. The board itself does not have audio out or audio in. On the Galileo Gen 1 board, the 3.5 mm connector is to connect to the host computer. So you'll need the following two pieces of hardware:

- A USB device that supports microphone in and speaker out. These are inexpensive and can be purchased at any online electronics outlet. Refer to the following image:

- A powered speaker that can plug into the USB device. Again, these are available online or at any audio store. Refer to the following image:

Make sure the speaker is powered because your board will generally not be able to drive a passive speaker with enough power for your applications. The speaker can use either internal battery power, or an externally powered USB hub.

Hooking up the hardware to make an input sound

For this task, you are going to hook up your hardware so that you can record and play sound. To do this, assemble your Galileo and the components. Plug in the LAN cable, or connect via the wireless adapter. Plug in the microphone or speaker USB device. Also, plug in your speakers and the microphone. Plug in the power, as well as the UART connector. The entire system should look like the following image:

Plug in the power. Once the terminal window comes up, log in with your user
name and password. Now type in cat /proc/asound/cards. The Galileo will tell
you what sound card it sees attached. You should see a response that resembles the
following screenshot:

```
user@Galileo:~$ cat /proc/asound/cards
 0 [Device         ]: USB-Audio - C-Media USB Audio Device
                      C-Media USB Audio Device at usb-0000:00:14.4-1, full speed
user@Galileo:~$
```

There is only one audio device, your USB audio plugin. First, let's play some music to test that the USB sound device is working. You'll need to configure your system to look for your USB audio plugin and use it as the default sound device to play and record sound. To do this, you'll need to add a couple of libraries to your system. The first is **Advanced Linux Sound Architecture** (**ALSA**). It is going to enable your sound system on the Galileo. Perform the following steps:

1. Firstly, install two libraries associated with ALSA by typing `sudo apt-get install alsa-base alsa-utils`. As a reminder, you need to have a network connection to download new packages, and apt-get will search the default package repository by name.

2. Then, also install some files that help provide the sound library by typing `sudo apt-get install libasound2-dev`.

If your system already contains these libraries, Linux will simply tell you that they are already installed or that they are up-to-date. After installing both libraries, reboot your Galileo. It takes time, and is not always required, but the system often needs a reboot after new libraries or hardware are installed.

Using an application

Now you'll use an application named `alsamixer` to control the volume of both the input and the output of our USB sound card. Perform the following steps:

1. Type `alsamixer` on the prompt. You should see a screen that looks like the following screenshot:

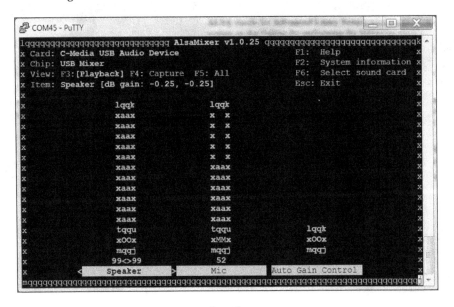

2. You can use the arrow keys to set the volume for both the speakers and the microphone. Use the *M* key to unmute the microphone. In the preceding screenshot, **MM** is mute and ∞ is unmute.

3. Let's make sure your system knows about your USB sound device. At the prompt, type `sudo aplay -l`. You should now see a screen resembling the following screenshot:

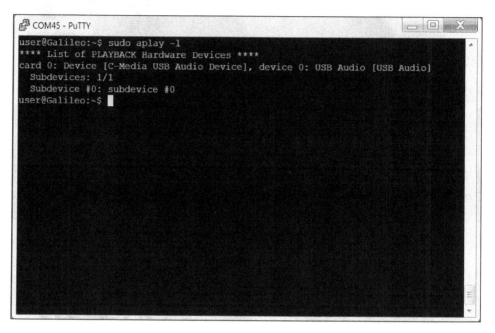

Now that you have some sound hardware, let's first record some sound. To do this, you're going to use the `arecord` program. At the prompt, type `arecord -d 5 -r 48000 test.wav`. This will record five seconds of sound at a 48,000 Hz sample rate and save it to a file called `test.wav`.

Once you have typed the command, either speak into the microphone or make some other recognizable sound. You should see the following output in the terminal:

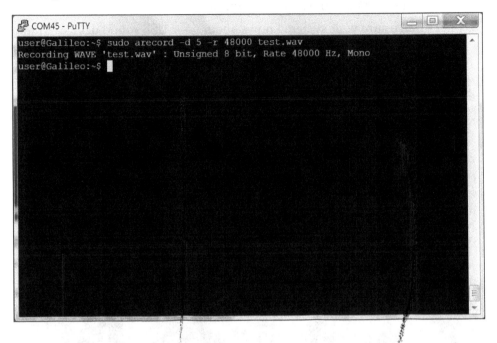

Once you create the file, play it with `aplay`. Type `sudo aplay test.wav` and you should hear the recording. If you can't hear your recording, check `alsamixer` to make sure your speakers and microphone are both unmuted.

Now you can play music or other sound files using your Galileo. You can change the volume of your speaker and record your voice or other sounds on the system. You're ready for the next step.

Using Espeak to allow our projects to respond in a robot voice

Sound is an important tool in our robotic toolkit, but you will want to do more than just record and play your voice. Let's allow your robot to speak. You're going to start by enabling Espeak, an open-source application that provides us with a computer voice. Download the Espeak library by typing `sudo apt-get install espeak`. The download might take a while, but the prompt will reappear when it is complete. Now let's see if your Galileo has a voice. Type the `sudo espeak "hello"` command. The speaker should emit a computer-voiced hello. If it does not, check the speakers and volume level.

Now that you have a computer voice, you might want to customize it. Espeak offers a fairly complete set of customization features, including a large number of languages, voices, and other options. To access these, you can type in the options at the command-line prompt. For example, type in `espeak -v+f3 "hello"` and you should hear a female voice. You can add a Scottish accent by typing `espeak -ven-sc+f3 "hello"`. The command line arguments that are available for Espeak are documented at `http://espeak.sourceforge.net/commands.html`. Once you have selected the kind of voice you'd like for your projects, you can set it as the default, so you don't always have to include it in the command line.

To set the default, go to the default file definition for `espeak`, which is in the `//usr/lib/arm-linux-gnueabihf/espeak-data/voices` directory. The default file is the one that `espeak` uses to choose a voice. To get your desired voice, say one with a female tone, you are going to copy a file into the default file. The file, that is, the female tone, is in the `!v` directory. Type `\!v` whenever you want to specify this directory. We need to type the `\` character because the `!` character is a special character in Linux; if we want to use it as a regular character, we need to put a `\` character before it. Before starting the process, copy the current default file into a file named `default.old`, so it can be retrieved later, if needed. The next step is to copy the `f3` voice as your default file. Type the `sudo cp ./\!v/f3 default` command. This has all the settings for your female voice. Now you can simply type `espeak` and the desired text. You will now get your female computer voice.

Now your project can speak. Simply type espeak followed by the text you want to speak in quotes and out comes your speech. If you want to read an entire text file, you can do that as well using the -f option and then typing the name of the file. Try this by using your editor to create a text file called speak.txt; then type the espeak -f speak.txt command.

There are lots of choices with respect to the voices you might use with espeak. Feel free to play around and choose your favorite. Then edit the default file to set it to that voice. However, don't expect that you'll get the kind of voices that you hear from computers in the movies. Those are actors and not computers; one day, though, we will hopefully get to the point where computers will sound a lot more like real people.

Summary

Now your project can speak. You can use this later when you want to interface with your project without using the display. You should also feel more comfortable installing new hardware and software in your system. In the next chapter, you'll add capability that will allow your robots to see and use vision to track objects, or motion, or whatever else your robot needs to track.

Index

Thank you for buying
Intel Galileo Essentials

About Packt Publishing

Packt, pronounced 'packed', published its first book, *Mastering phpMyAdmin for Effective MySQL Management*, in April 2004, and subsequently continued to specialize in publishing highly focused books on specific technologies and solutions.

Our books and publications share the experiences of your fellow IT professionals in adapting and customizing today's systems, applications, and frameworks. Our solution-based books give you the knowledge and power to customize the software and technologies you're using to get the job done. Packt books are more specific and less general than the IT books you have seen in the past. Our unique business model allows us to bring you more focused information, giving you more of what you need to know, and less of what you don't.

Packt is a modern yet unique publishing company that focuses on producing quality, cutting-edge books for communities of developers, administrators, and newbies alike. For more information, please visit our website at www.packtpub.com.

About Packt Open Source

In 2010, Packt launched two new brands, Packt Open Source and Packt Enterprise, in order to continue its focus on specialization. This book is part of the Packt Open Source brand, home to books published on software built around open source licenses, and offering information to anybody from advanced developers to budding web designers. The Open Source brand also runs Packt's Open Source Royalty Scheme, by which Packt gives a royalty to each open source project about whose software a book is sold.

Writing for Packt

We welcome all inquiries from people who are interested in authoring. Book proposals should be sent to author@packtpub.com. If your book idea is still at an early stage and you would like to discuss it first before writing a formal book proposal, then please contact us; one of our commissioning editors will get in touch with you.

We're not just looking for published authors; if you have strong technical skills but no writing experience, our experienced editors can help you develop a writing career, or simply get some additional reward for your expertise.

Arduino Robotic Projects

ISBN: 978-1-78398-982-9   Paperback: 240 pages

Build awesome and complex robots with the power of Arduino

1. Develop a series of exciting robots that can sail, go under water, and fly.

2. Simple, easy-to-understand instructions to program Arduino.

3. Effectively control the movements of all types of motors using Arduino.

4. Use sensors, GSP, and a magnetic compass to give your robot direction and make it lifelike.

Arduino Home Automation Projects

ISBN: 978-1-78398-606-4   Paperback: 132 pages

Automate your home using the powerful Arduino platform

1. Interface home automation components with Arduino.

2. Automate your projects to communicate wirelessly using XBee, Bluetooth and WiFi.

3. Build seven exciting, instruction-based home automation projects with Arduino in no time.

Please check **www.PacktPub.com** for information on our titles

Internet of Things with the Arduino Yún

ISBN: 978-1-78328-800-7   Paperback: 112 pages

Projects to help you build a world of smarter things

1. Learn how to interface various sensors and actuators to the Arduino Yún and send this data in the cloud.

2. Explore the possibilities offered by the Internet of Things by using the Arduino Yún to upload measurements to Google Docs, upload pictures to Dropbox, and send live video streams to YouTube.

3. Learn how to use the Arduino Yún as the brain of a robot that can be completely controlled via Wi-Fi.

Raspberry Pi Home Automation with Arduino

ISBN: 978-1-84969-586-2   Paperback: 176 pages

Automate your home with a set of exciting projects for the Raspberry Pi!

1. Learn how to dynamically adjust your living environment with detailed step-by-step examples.

2. Discover how you can utilize the combined power of the Raspberry Pi and Arduino for your own projects.

3. Revolutionize the way you interact with your home on a daily basis.

Please check **www.PacktPub.com** for information on our titles